The Peni2Dollarzfx Day Trading Handguide

Leguan Penigo

The Peni2Dollarzfx Day Trading Handguide

Published by BooxAi

ISBN: 978-965-578-641-5

The Peni2Dollarzfx Day Trading Handguide

Leguan Penigo

Contents

Preface

I began my journey of learning how to day trade in October 2019. I distinctly remember taking an interest in trading before the whole AMC, GameStop, and Dogecoin craze. It was during this time I experienced some real gains and profits, along with many others in the market. I personally experienced first-hand not only the infinite freedom, possibilities, and benefits of investing, but more importantly, the necessity of needing to learn how to day trade correctly. I became obsessed with everything day trading. I easily invested more than 10,000 hours on the charts, viewing YouTube videos, testing strategies, and learning about lot sizes, brokers, indicators and so much more.

I created this handbook with the most novice trader in mind. The content and material offered in this handbook ranges from those who have placed over a thousand trades in the market to those who have never placed a trade at all, and everyone in between. This handbook is intended as a quick reference user guide for any aspiring new trader who wishes to get started and any more-seasoned trader who is looking to gain a deeper understanding of the many concepts involved in day trading.

In my opinion, trading is truly the epitome of owning a superior, white-collar skill. If you desire to possess a skill that will always be yours, that is recession-proof, and has limitless earning potential, this handbook was made with you in mind.

Remember that trading is the art of taking a position in the market that limits losses in the event of it occurring, while at the same time exposing your position to unlimited profits or gains.

Trading is not for everyone. My past results are not indicative of anyone's future performance or results. The images and illustrations I use in this user guide are examples of my past results and are by no means financial advice. Please trade responsibly.

Disclaimer: This guide is not intended to be an all-inclusive book on everything related to day trading. However, the objective of this guide is to assist any beginning or aspiring trader, in better understanding the fundamental concepts. I found these concepts valuable in supporting me to be consistent in my trading journey. Many of the concepts in this hand guide are in bulleted lists and are oversimplified to better explain these concepts and to demonstrate how to practically apply them.

SECTION 1: Introduction to Forex

What is forex? How does one make money in forex?

Before I explain forex and what it is, remember it's just one specific type of financial market. There are various financial markets in trading. For example, there is the foreign exchange market, cryptocurrency, and stock market, to name a few. If you travel to another country, you usually have to find a currency exchange booth at the airport. You exchange the money you have in your wallet into the currency of the country you are visiting.

Forex is short for foreign exchange. It is the global financial market that allows someone to trade currencies. If you place a trade that one currency will be stronger versus the other currency and you are correct, you can make a profit. The opposite is true, too. If you pick the currency strength to increase but it goes down, you may lose considerably. The value of anything traded in the financial markets is never constant. It is always fluid, always fluctuating up and down and even sideways. The value of the dollar fluctuates constantly. As an experienced and disciplined trader with a proven, consistent systematic approach to the market, you can garner the skills to unlock the edge you need to gain financial freedom.

The key to trading, in my opinion, is that trading is the art of structuring your position in the market so that you minimize losses while exposing yourself to great gains or profits. To do this, I practice risking only 1% of the position in a trade. This practice always limits me to only a 1% loss.

Forex refers to the global decentralized market where currencies are bought, sold, and exchanged. It is the largest and most fluid financial market in the world. Daily trading volumes exceed trillions of dollars. Forex trading involves speculating on the relative value of different currencies with the aim of profiting from the fluctuations in exchange rates.

In the forex market, participants (including banks, financial institutions, corporations, governments, and individual traders) engage in currency trading. The primary purpose of forex trading is to facilitate international trade and investment by enabling the conversion of one currency into another.

Key Features of the Forex Market:

Global Market: The forex market operates 24 hours a day, five days a week, allowing participants from around the world to trade currencies. It is a decentralized market; there is no physical location or central exchange. Instead, trading occurs electronically over-the-counter (OTC) through a network of financial institutions, brokers, and electronic trading platforms.

Currency Pairs: Forex trading involves trading currency pairs which represent the value of one currency relative to another. The most commonly traded currency pairs include the major currencies such as the U.S. dollar (USD), euro

(EUR), Japanese yen (JPY), British pound (GBP), Swiss franc (CHF), Canadian dollar (CAD), Australian dollar (AUD), and New Zealand dollar (NZD).

Exchange Rate Fluctuations: The forex market is characterized by constant exchange rate fluctuations. These fluctuations occur due to various factors such as economic indicators, geopolitical events, interest rates, political developments, and market sentiment. Traders aim to predict the direction of these exchange rate movements and take positions accordingly.

Leverage: Forex trading often involves the use of leverage, which allows traders to control larger positions with a fraction of the capital required. Leverage is provided by brokers. It enables traders to amplify their potential profits, but it can also magnify their losses. It is important to note that leverage should be used with caution and proper risk management techniques.

High Liquidity: The forex market's immense size and high trading volumes result in high liquidity; there is generally a large number of buyers and sellers available at any given time. This provides traders with the ability to enter and exit trades quickly, ensuring that they can execute their desired transactions without significant price slippage (the difference between the expected price of a trade and the price at which the trade is executed).

Trading Strategies: Forex trading involves various trading strategies, including technical analysis, fundamental analysis, and sentiment analysis. Traders use charts, indicators, economic data, news releases, and other tools to make informed trading decisions.

Forex trading offers opportunities for both short-term speculation and long-term investment. Traders can participate directly through forex brokers or indirectly through financial derivatives such as forex futures contracts, options, and contracts for difference (CFDs).

It is important to note that forex trading carries risks, including the potential for significant losses, due to the inherent volatility and leverage involved.

Traders should acquire: 1.) A solid understanding of the forex or financial market(s), 2.) Develop an effective trading strategy, and 3.) Exercise proper risk management techniques before engaging in trading any asset.

SECTION 2: Currency Pairs / Currency Exchange

A currency pair, also known as a forex pair or currency exchange pair, is a quote of the relative value of one currency against another in the foreign exchange (forex) market. It represents the exchange rate between two currencies and is used to facilitate currency trading.

Currency pairs are typically denoted by a three-letter

code, with the first two letters representing the base currency and the last letter representing the quote currency. The base currency is the currency you are buying or selling, and the quote currency is the currency you are using to compare it to.

For example, in the currency pair EUR/USD, the euro (EUR) is the base currency, and the US dollar (USD) is the quote currency. This pair represents the exchange rate of how many US dollars are needed to purchase one euro.

Currency pairs are quoted, or listed, into two price categories: the bid price and the ask price. The bid price is the price at which the market is willing to buy the base currency in exchange for the quote currency. The ask price is the price at which the market is willing to sell the base currency in exchange for the quote currency. The difference between the bid and ask prices is known as the spread.

Currency pairs can be categorized into three main types:

Major Pairs: Major currency pairs are the most actively traded and widely recognized pairs in the forex market. They involve the US dollar and a currency from a major global economy. Examples include EUR/USD, GBP/USD, USD/JPY, USD/CHF, and USD/CAD.

Minor or Cross Pairs: Minor currency pairs, also known as cross pairs, do not involve the US dollar. They consist of two major currencies from economies other than the United States. Examples include EUR/GBP, GBP/JPY, AUD/CAD, and NZD/JPY.

Exotic Pairs: Exotic currency pairs involve one major currency and one currency from an emerging or less frequently traded economy. They typically have lower liquidity and higher spreads compared to major and minor pairs. Examples include USD/ZAR, USD/TRY, EUR/TRY, and GBP/MXN.

Currency pairs are traded in the forex market which operates globally, around the clock. Traders and investors engage in currency exchange to speculate on exchange rate movements, hedge against currency risk, facilitate international trade, or engage in carry trades to take advantage of interest rate differentials between currencies.

Understanding currency pairs and their dynamics is crucial for participants in the forex market to make informed trading decisions and manage currency-related exposures.

SECTION 3: Cryptocurrency

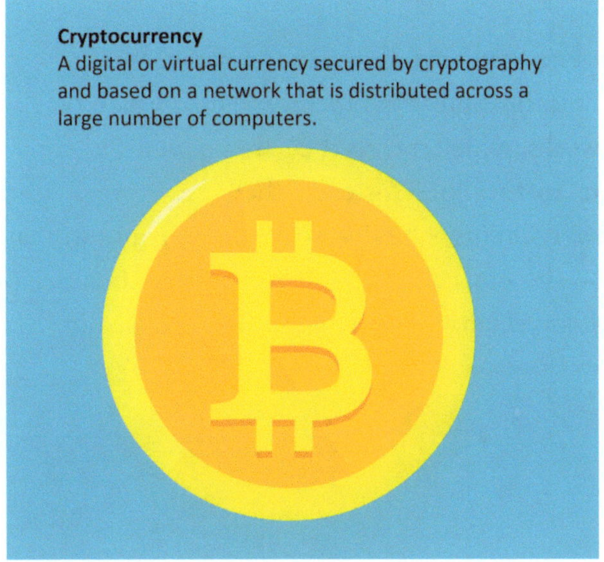

Cryptocurrency – A cryptocurrency, crypto, is an umbrella term for a new kind of digital money that relies on a combination of technologies that allows it to exist outside the control of central authorities like governments and banks. Cryptocurrencies have no physical form. There are no dollar bills or metal coins. They are completely digital, meaning they're literally just lines of computer code. This means that, unlike fiat currencies, cryptocurrencies are not controlled by a central authority; there is no bank or government behind them. This defining feature of cryptocurrencies is known as decentralization. Units of a cryptocurrency are generated based on predetermined rules written in code which are executed by software.

BTCUSD (Bitcoin)

ETHUSD (Ethereum)

XRPUSD (Ripple)

Note: Each of these crypto assets is traded against the US Dollar.

Key Features of Cryptocurrencies:

Decentralization: Cryptocurrencies operate on decentralized networks, which means they are not controlled by a single entity or institution. Instead, they rely on a distributed network of computers (nodes) that maintain and validate transactions on the blockchain. This decentralized nature provides transparency, security, and resistance to censorship.

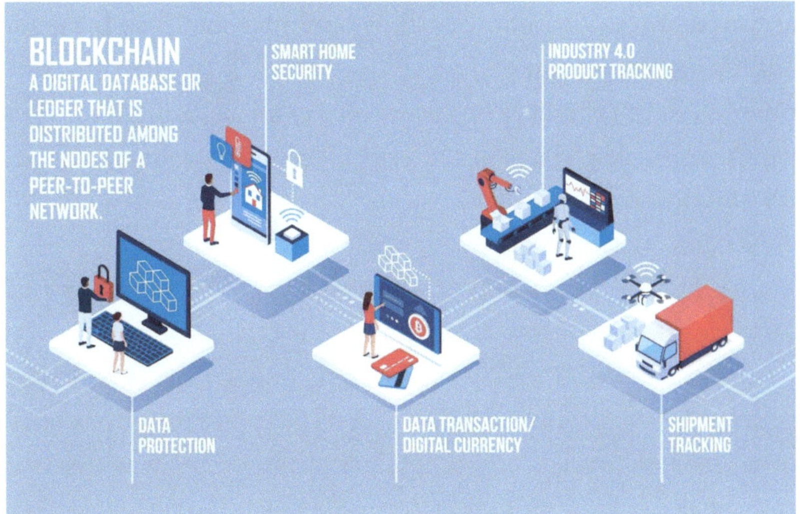

Blockchain Technology: Cryptocurrencies are built on blockchain technology, which is a distributed ledger that records and verifies all transactions across the network. The blockchain ensures transparency, immutability, and integrity of the transaction history. Each transaction is grouped into blocks and linked together in a chronological chain.

Cryptographic Security: Cryptocurrencies employ cryptographic techniques to secure transactions and control the creation of new units. Public-key cryptography is used to encrypt and verify transactions, ensuring the authenticity and integrity of the information exchanged.

Limited Supply: Many cryptocurrencies have a predetermined supply cap, meaning there is a maximum number of units that can ever be created. This scarcity can contribute to their value proposition and potential price appreciation over time. Bitcoin, for example, has a maximum supply of 21 million coins.

Pseudonymity and Privacy: Cryptocurrency transactions

are often pseudonymous, as they are associated with digital addresses rather than real-world identities. While the transaction details are publicly recorded on the blockchain, the link to personal information is not always readily apparent. However, it's important to note that some cryptocurrencies focus on enhancing privacy features.

Utility and Use Cases: Cryptocurrencies serve various purposes beyond being a medium of exchange. They can be used for remittances, decentralized finance (DeFi), smart contracts, decentralized applications (DApps), digital identity management, and more. Each cryptocurrency may have a specific use case or unique features.

Volatility: Cryptocurrencies are known for their price volatility, with significant price fluctuations occurring over short periods. This volatility can present both opportunities and risks for investors and traders.

Cryptocurrencies have gained attention for their potential to revolutionize various industries and challenge traditional financial systems. However, it's important to recognize that investing in cryptocurrencies carries risks, including price volatility, regulatory uncertainty, technological challenges, and potential security vulnerabilities. It is advisable to conduct thorough research and exercise caution when trading in the cryptocurrency market.

SECTION 4: Stocks and Other Commodities

Stock
A stock, also known as equity, is a security that represents the ownership of a fraction of the issuing corporation.

Stocks and commodities are both types of financial instruments that are traded in various markets. However, there are fundamental differences between them in terms of their nature, underlying assets, and the way they are traded.

STOCKS:

A stock, also known as equity, is a security that represents the ownership of a fraction of the issuing corporation. Units of stock are called shares. They entitle the owner to a proportion of the corporation's assets and profits equal to how much stock they own. Stocks are bought and sold predominantly on stock exchanges and are the foundation of many individual investors' portfolios. Stock trades have to conform to government regulations meant to protect investors from fraudulent practices.

Stock Basics:

Nature: Stocks, also known as shares or equities, represent ownership in a company. When an individual or entity purchases stocks of a company, they become shareholders and have a claim on the company's assets and earnings.

Underlying Asset: Stocks are based on the ownership of publicly traded companies. Each stock represents a fractional ownership interest in the company, and shareholders have certain rights, such as voting rights and the right to receive dividends.

Trading Market: Stocks are primarily traded on stock exchanges, such as the New York Stock Exchange (NYSE) or National Association of Securities Dealers Automatic Quotation (NASDAQ). These exchanges provide a platform for buyers and sellers to trade stocks. Stock prices are influenced by factors such as the company's financial performance, industry trends, and overall market conditions.

Value Determination: The value of stocks is primarily driven by the company's financial performance, including factors such as revenue growth, profitability, and future prospects. Market sentiment and investor perceptions also play a significant role in determining stock prices.

Investment Strategy: Investors can buy and hold stocks for the long term as a means of participating in a company's growth and receiving dividends. Additionally, traders engage in short-term buying and selling of stocks to capitalize on price fluctuations.

Examples are the following:

AAPL (Apple Inc)

AMZN (Amazon.com)

GOOGL (Alphabet Inc "Google")

NFLX (Netflix Inc)

COMMODITIES:

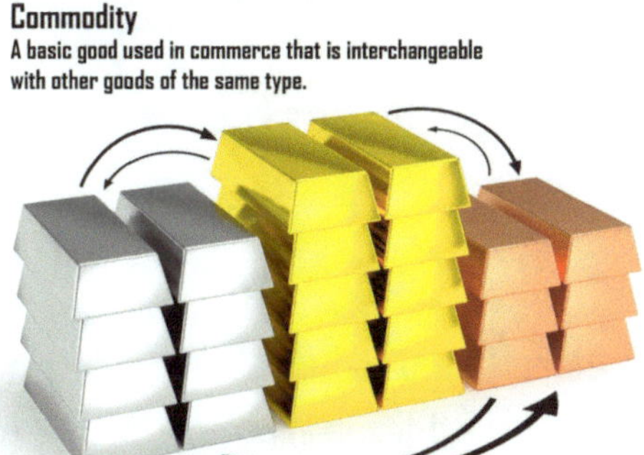

Nature: Commodities are raw materials or primary goods that can be bought and sold, usually in large quantities. They can include physical substances like agricultural products (wheat, corn), metals (gold, silver), energy resources (crude oil, natural gas), or soft commodities (coffee, cotton).

Gold can be traded on the exchange. XAUUSD (GOLD Spot/US Dollar)

Underlying Asset: Commodities are based on physical goods or resources. They represent the ownership or right to take delivery of a specific quantity of the underlying commodity.

Trading Market: Commodities are traded on specialized exchanges such as the Chicago Mercantile Exchange (CME) or Intercontinental Exchange (ICE). Commodities can be traded in the spot market, where immediate delivery takes place, or in the futures market, where contracts for future delivery are bought and sold.

Value Determination: The value of commodities is influenced by factors such as supply and demand dynamics, geopolitical events, weather conditions, and global economic trends.

For example, the price of crude oil is influenced by factors such as production levels, global demand, and geopolitical tensions.

Investment Strategy: Investors in commodities can take physical possession of the commodities or invest through derivatives such as futures contracts or exchange-traded funds (ETFs). Commodities can provide diversification benefits to an investment portfolio and can be used as a hedge against inflation or as speculative investments.

In summary, stocks represent ownership in companies and are traded on stock exchanges, while commodities represent physical goods or resources and are traded on specialized exchanges. A stock's value is based on the performance of the underlying company, while a commodity's value is driven by supply and demand dynamics. Both stocks and commodities offer investment opportunities but differ in their underlying assets, trading markets, and value determinants.

SECTION 5: Indices/Indexes

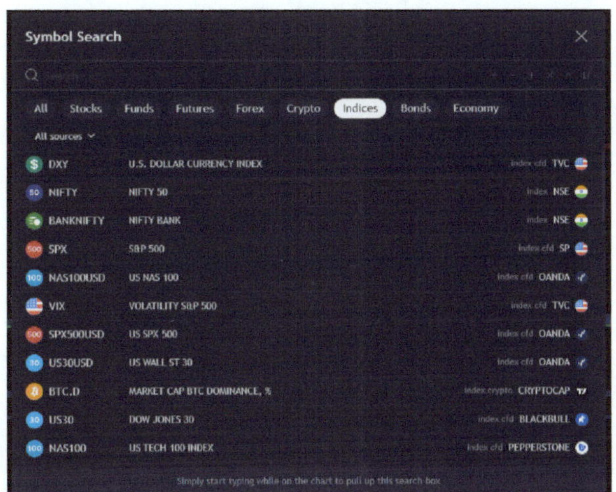

Index / Indices – An index is a method to track the performance of a group of assets in a standardized way. Indexes typically measure the performance of a basket of securities intended to replicate a certain area of the market. These could be constructed as a broad-based index that captures the entire market, such as the Standard and Poor's

500 or Dow Jones Industrial Average (DJIA), or more specialized such as indexes that track a particular industry or segment such as the Russell 2000 Index, which tracks only small-cap stocks.

Key Characteristics of Indices:

Composition: An index is composed of a predefined selection of securities or assets that meet certain criteria. For example, a stock index may include a specific set of stocks that meet size, liquidity, and other eligibility criteria. The composition of an index can vary based on factors like market capitalization, industry sector, geographic region, or other specific criteria.

Weighting Methodology: Indices use different weighting methodologies to determine the influence of each constituent asset on the overall index value. Common weighting methods include market capitalization weighting (assigning weights based on the market value of each constituent), equal weighting (assigning equal weights to each constituent), or price weighting (assigning weights based on the price of each constituent).

Performance Measurement: Indices are designed to track and measure the performance of the underlying assets over a specific period. They provide a reference point for investors to evaluate the performance of their portfolios, compare investment returns, and assess market trends.

Calculation Method: Index values are calculated using specific mathematical formulas. These formulas can vary depending on the index provider and the specific index methodology. Generally, index values are calculated using a weighted average or market value-based formula.

Representative of a Market or Sector: Indices are often designed to represent a broader market, specific industry sector, or asset class. For example, the S&P 500 index represents the performance of the largest 500 publicly traded companies in the United States, while the FTSE 100 index represents the performance of the 100 largest companies listed on the London Stock Exchange.

Benchmarking: Indices are commonly used as benchmarks for measuring the performance of investment portfolios or financial products. Investors and fund managers often compare their investment returns against relevant indices to assess the success of their strategies or funds.

Examples are the following:

DE30EUR (German 30, DAX)

UK100GB (UK 100)

US 30 (Dow Jones Industrial Average)

NAS 100 (US NAS 100)

SPX500 (S&P 500)

FTSE 100

Nikkei 225

Hang Seng Index

Indices provide a snapshot of market performance, allow for the creation of index-based investment products like index funds or exchange-traded funds (ETFs), and serve as a tool for investment analysis, risk management, and portfolio diversification. They are widely used in financial markets to track market trends, evaluate investment performance, and make informed investment decisions.

SECTION 6: Mutual Funds

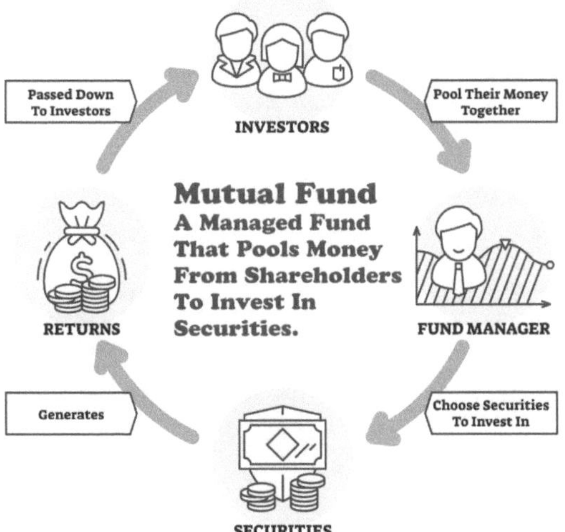

Do not confuse mutual funds and indices. Mutual funds are investment vehicles that pool money from multiple investors to invest in a diversified portfolio of securities such as stocks, bonds, and other assets. They are managed by professional fund managers or investment companies.

Here are some key points about mutual funds:

Diversification: Mutual funds offer diversification by investing in a wide range of securities. By spreading investments across different asset classes and industries, mutual funds aim to reduce risk and provide investors with exposure to a diversified portfolio.

Professional Management: Mutual funds are managed by experienced investment professionals who make decisions regarding asset allocation, security selection, and portfolio rebalancing. The fund manager's goal is to generate returns that align with the fund's stated investment objective.

Investment Objectives and Strategies: Mutual funds are structured with specific investment objectives and strategies. These can vary, such as growth funds that aim for capital appreciation, income funds that focus on generating regular income, or balanced funds that seek a mix of growth and income. Each mutual fund has a stated investment strategy that guides its portfolio composition and investment decisions.

Net Asset Value (NAV): The Net Asset Value represents the per-share value of a mutual fund's assets minus liabilities. The NAV is calculated at the end of each trading day and is used to determine the price at which investors can buy or sell mutual fund shares. Mutual fund shares are typically bought and sold at their NAV, which fluctuates based on the performance of the underlying securities held by the fund.

Liquidity: Mutual funds offer liquidity, allowing investors to buy or sell shares on any business day at the fund's NAV. This provides flexibility for investors to enter or exit their investments without the need to directly trade the underlying securities.

Fees and Expenses: Mutual funds charge fees and expenses for management, administration, and other operational costs. These fees are typically expressed as an annual percentage of the fund's assets and are deducted from the fund's returns. Common types of fees include management fees, administrative fees, and 12b-1 fees (for marketing and distribution).

Regulatory Oversight: Mutual funds are subject to regulatory oversight and must comply with regulations set by financial authorities in the countries where they operate. In the United States, mutual funds are regulated by the Securities and Exchange Commission (SEC) under the Investment Company Act of 1940.

Investor Accessibility: Mutual funds are accessible to individual investors with various investment amounts. They provide an avenue for individuals to participate in the financial markets without needing to directly manage a diversified portfolio of securities.

It's important to carefully review a mutual fund's prospectus, which provides detailed information about the fund's investment objective, strategy, risks, fees, and historical performance. Understanding these factors can help investors make informed decisions about investing in mutual funds that align with their financial goals and risk tolerance.

SECTION 7: Top-Down Analysis

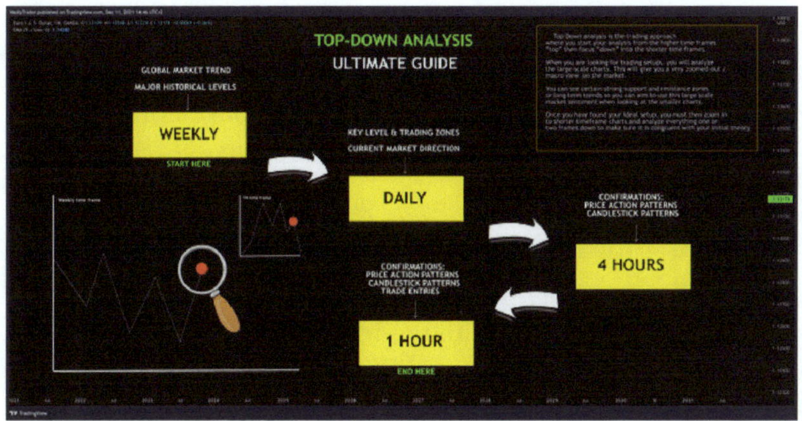

The process of top-down analysis typically involves the following steps:

Macro-level Analysis: The analysis begins by assessing the overall macroeconomic environment and global market trends. This includes studying factors such as GDP growth, interest rates, inflation, fiscal and monetary policies, geopolitical events, and global economic indicators. The objective is to understand the broader economic conditions that can impact various industries and sectors.

Industry Analysis: Once the macroeconomic factors are evaluated, the focus shifts to specific industries or sectors. The goal is to identify sectors that are expected to perform well or have favorable conditions based on the macroeconomic analysis. Factors considered include industry growth rates, regulatory environment, technological advancements, competitive landscape, and consumer trends.

Company Analysis: After identifying attractive sectors, the analysis narrows down to individual companies within those sectors. Fundamental analysis is conducted on each company to assess their financial health, competitive position, management quality, growth prospects, and valuation. This may involve examining financial statements, conducting ratio analysis, evaluating earnings reports, and considering qualitative factors.

Security Selection: Based on the company analysis, specific securities or investments are selected. This can include individual stocks, bonds, mutual funds, or exchange-traded funds (ETFs) that align with the identified sectors and companies with favorable prospects. Factors such as risk tolerance, investment objectives, and time horizon are considered in the selection process.

Portfolio Construction: Finally, the selected securities are combined to construct a diversified portfolio that aligns with the investor's goals and risk preferences. The portfolio may be weighted based on the attractiveness of different sectors, asset classes, or specific investment opportunities identified during the analysis.

The top-down analysis approach recognizes that macroeconomic factors can significantly influence sector performance, which, in turn, impacts individual companies and their securities. By starting with a broad analysis and gradually drilling down to specific investments, investors aim to identify opportunities and manage risk in a systematic manner.

Top-down analysis is just one approach to financial analysis, and investors may also employ a bottom-up approach, which focuses primarily on analyzing individual companies and their financials before considering broader market trends. Many investors use a combination of both approaches to make informed investment decisions.

Top-down analysis, in simple terms, is a method used to make investment decisions by looking at the big picture before focusing on the details. It involves considering the overall economic conditions, industry trends, and then selecting specific investments.

Imagine you want to plan a trip to a new city. Instead of randomly picking places to visit, you start by researching the country or region's overall weather, culture, and popular attractions. This is like the macro-level analysis in top-down analysis.

Once you have an idea of the country or region you want to visit, you narrow down your focus to specific cities or areas. You consider factors like local customs, safety, tourist attractions, and local cuisine. This is similar to the industry analysis in top-down analysis.

After deciding on the city or area to visit, you start looking for specific hotels, restaurants, and activities that match your preferences and budget. You consider factors like hotel ratings, customer reviews, menu options, and prices. This is similar to the company analysis in top-down analysis.

Finally, you put together your itinerary by combining the selected hotels, restaurants, and activities to create a well-rounded and enjoyable trip. This is like constructing a diversified investment portfolio based on the chosen investments from the top-down analysis.

In summary, top-down analysis is like planning a trip by starting with the big picture (macro-level analysis), narrowing down to specific destinations (industry analysis), selecting individual accommodations and activities (company analysis), and then organizing them into a cohesive plan (portfolio construction).

SECTION 8: Candlestick Anatomy

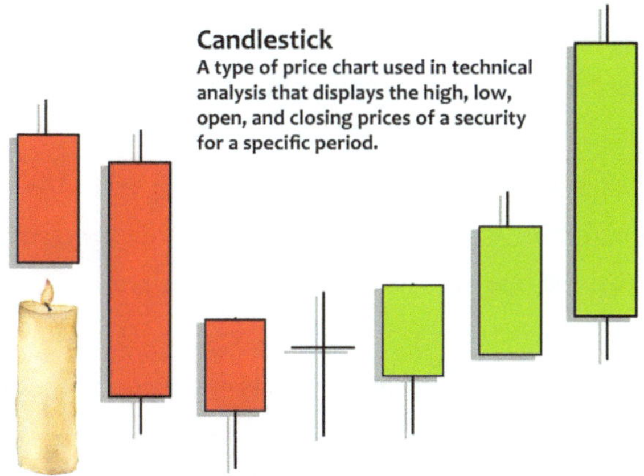

Candlestick anatomy refers to the components and characteristics of a candlestick chart, which is a popular form of price representation in technical analysis. Candlestick charts provide valuable information about the price action of a financial asset over a given period. Each individual candlestick represents a specific time frame (e.g., one day, one hour) and consists of four main elements:

Body: The body of a candlestick represents the price range between the opening and closing prices of the asset during the given time period. It is represented by a rectangular shape. If the closing price is higher than the opening price, the body is typically filled or colored, indicating a bullish (upward) candlestick. Inversely, if the closing price is lower than the opening price, the body is usually hollow or colored differently, indicating a bearish (downward) candlestick.

Wick/Shadow: The wick or shadow of a candlestick represents the price extremes reached during the time period. It includes two components:

Upper Wick/Shadow: The upper wick extends from the top of the body to the highest price reached during the period. It indicates the maximum price reached by the asset before pulling back.

Lower Wick/Shadow: The lower wick extends from the bottom of the body to the lowest price reached during the period. It represents the minimum price reached by the asset before bouncing back.

Open Price: The open price is represented by a horizontal dash or a small tick on the left side of the body. It indicates the price at which the asset opened at the beginning of the time period.

Close Price: The close price is represented by a horizontal dash or a small tick on the right side of the body. It indicates the price at which the asset closed at the end of the time period.

Long bodies show strong buying or selling. The longer the

body is, the more intense the buying or selling pressure. This means that either buyers or sellers were stronger and took control.

By analyzing the relationship between the body, wicks, and open/close prices of candlesticks, traders can gain insights into the market sentiment and potential price reversals. Different candlestick patterns, such as doji, hammer, engulfing, and shooting star, provide further indications about potential trends and market reversals.

It's important to note that the interpretation of candlestick patterns should not rely solely on one or two candles but rather on observing patterns and their context in the broader price chart. Traders often use candlestick analysis in conjunction with other technical indicators and tools to make more informed trading decisions.

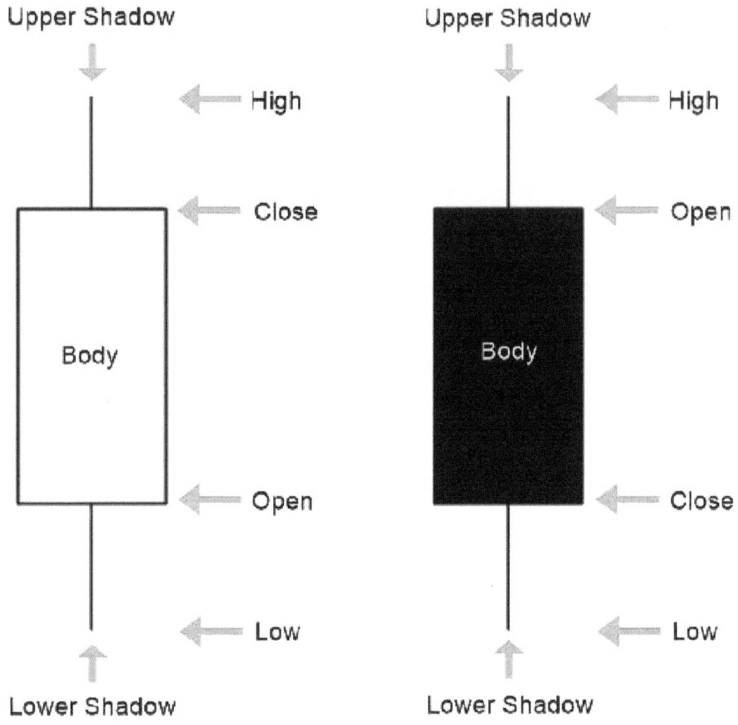
Upper Shadow
High
Close
Body
Open
Low
Lower Shadow
Upper Shadow
High
Open
Body
Close
Low
Lower Shadow

SECTION 9: Price Action

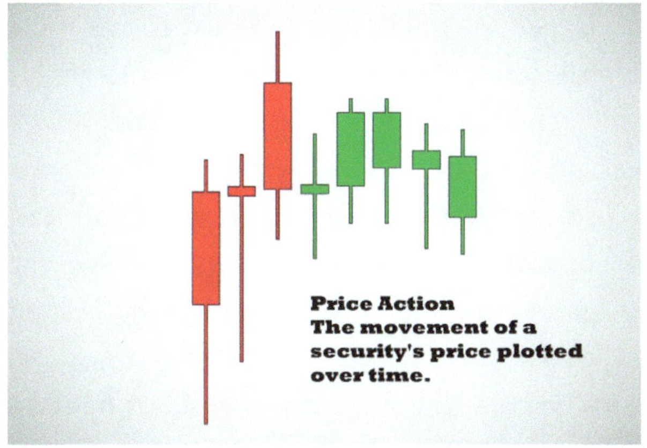

Price action refers to the movement and behavior of the price of a financial instrument, such as a stock, currency pair, or commodity, on a trading chart. Price action trading is a trading methodology that focuses on analyzing and making trading decisions based primarily on the patterns and movements of the price itself, rather than relying heavily on indicators or other external factors.

Price action traders believe that all relevant information regarding a financial instrument's price is reflected in its historical price movements. They study patterns, trends, support and resistance levels, chart formations, and other price-related factors to identify potential trading opportunities and make informed trading decisions.

Here are some key aspects of price action and price action trading:

Candlestick Charts: Price action analysis is often conducted using candlestick charts. Candlestick charts provide visual representations of price movements over a specific time period. Each candlestick displays the opening, closing, high, and low prices for the period, allowing traders to analyze the relationship between buyers and sellers during that time.

Patterns and Chart Formations: Price action traders look for specific patterns and chart formations that suggest potential market reversals, continuations, or trend strength. Examples of common price action patterns include pin bars, engulfing patterns, inside bars, and head and shoulders patterns. These patterns can provide signals for entry or exit points, as well as clues about market sentiment. Uptrends and Downtrends are examples of chart formations.

Support and Resistance Levels: Price action traders pay close attention to support and resistance levels on a chart. Support levels are price levels where buying interest is expected to be strong enough to prevent the price from falling further. On the other hand, resistance levels are price levels where selling pressure is expected to be strong enough to prevent the price from rising further. Traders use these levels to identify potential areas of price reversal or breakout.

Trend Analysis: Price action traders analyze the overall trend of the market and look for opportunities to trade in the direction of the prevailing trend. They identify higher highs and higher lows in an uptrend or lower highs and lower lows in a downtrend to confirm the direction of the market and make trading decisions accordingly.

Risk Management: Price action traders focus on effective risk management by placing stop-loss orders to limit potential losses and using proper position sizing techniques. They aim to identify favorable risk-reward ratios based on price action analysis and adjust their trade parameters accordingly.

Price action trading requires practice, experience, and discipline. Traders need to develop an understanding of various price patterns, support and resistance levels, and other aspects of price behavior. By observing and interpreting price action, traders aim to gain insights into the market's sentiment, make informed trading decisions, and potentially improve their trading results.

There are two primary methods used to analyze securities and make investment decisions: technical analysis and fundamental analysis.

SECTION 10: Technical Analysis

Technical analysis is by far the most single-handed advantage I use to approach the market when trading. It's not the only approach by any means, but 70% or more of my trades are determined by chart patterns, supply and demand areas or zones, and price action analysis, which is also known as "technical analysis." This process can appear very daunting and even complicated or confusing to learn at first, but I'm here to tell you that it can be done. Plus, it's totally worth it.

You must remember the financial markets, for the most part, function totally randomly. We'll talk more on that later. When you develop the discipline, along with technical skill, you develop that ever-so-necessary and needed .01% edge to make large financial gains in the market. It's this edge that enables you to remain a constant variable in a random equation.

I offer you this reminder: Think of the markets as always being fluid, constantly moving in either direction. When you apply a constant, strict set of rules, strategy, and risk management, you now position yourself to extract from the market at will. The goal is to limit your losses to a set amount on every trade and enable your profits to compound. That's truly all there is to it. Technical analysis simply offers you more of a predictive analysis that when supported by your rules and trading discipline can yield you unlimited profits for the remainder of your existence.

Technical analysis is used to evaluate and forecast future price movements of financial assets, such as stocks, currencies, commodities, and indices. It involves analyzing historical market data, primarily through the use of charts, patterns, and statistical indicators, to identify patterns, trends, and potential trading opportunities.

Technical analysis, as we know it today, was first introduced by Charles Dow and the Dow Theory in the late 1800s. Technical analysis has evolved to include hundreds of patterns and signals observed through years of research. Technical analysis is a trading discipline employed to evaluate investments and identify trading opportunities in price trends and patterns seen on charts.

Technical analysts believe past trading activity and price

changes of a security can be valuable indicators of the security's future price movements. Technical analysis may be contrasted with fundamental analysis which focuses on a company's financials rather than historical price patterns or stock trends.

Technical analysis tools are used to scrutinize the ways supply and demand for a security will affect changes in price, volume, and implied volatility. The analysis operates from the assumption that past trading activity and price changes of a security can be valuable indicators of the security's future price movements when paired with appropriate investing or trading rules. It is often used to generate short-term trading signals from various charting tools but can also help improve the evaluation of a security's strength or weakness relative to the broader market or one of its sectors. This information helps analysts improve their overall estimate of value.

Across the industry, there are hundreds of patterns and signals that have been developed by researchers to support technical analysis trading. Technical analysts have also developed numerous types of trading systems to help them forecast and trade on price movements. Some indicators are focused primarily on identifying the current market trend, including support and resistance areas, while others are focused on determining the strength of a trend and the likelihood of its continuation. Commonly used technical indicators and charting patterns include trendlines, channels, moving averages, and momentum indicators.

In general, technical analysts look at the following broad types of indicators:

Price trends

Chart patterns

Volume and momentum indicators
Oscillators
Moving averages
Support and resistance levels

Let's take a closer look at the key concepts of technical analysis:

Price Patterns: Technical analysts study price patterns, such as trendlines, support and resistance levels, chart patterns (e.g., head and shoulders, double top/bottom), and trend channels. These patterns provide insights into the potential direction of price movements.

Chart Patterns: Chart patterns, such as triangles, flags, pennants, and wedges, provide visual representations of price behavior. Traders analyze these patterns to anticipate future price movements and make trading decisions.

Trend Analysis: Technical analysis focuses on identifying trends, which represent the general direction of price movements. Trends can be bullish (upward), bearish (downward), or sideways (range-bound). Trend analysis helps traders determine the overall market sentiment and potential entry or exit points.

Indicators: Technical analysts use various indicators to assess market conditions and generate trading signals. Examples of indicators include moving averages, oscillators [e.g., Relative Strength Index (RSI), Moving Average Convergence and Divergence (MACD), Stochastic], volume indicators, and Bollinger Bands. Indicators help identify overbought or oversold conditions, momentum shifts, and trend strength.

Volume Analysis: Volume refers to the number of shares or contracts traded in a given period. Volume analysis helps traders assess the strength or weakness of a price move. High volume during price advances or declines can indicate the presence of significant buying or selling pressure.

Moving Averages: Moving averages are calculated by averaging the prices over a specified time period. They help smoothen out price fluctuations and identify the overall trend direction. Common types of moving averages include simple moving averages (SMA) and exponential moving averages (EMA).

Fibonacci Analysis: Fibonacci retracement and extension levels are derived from a mathematical sequence. Traders use these levels to identify potential support and resistance zones, as well as areas for price retracements or extensions.

Support and Resistance: Support levels are price levels where buying pressure is expected to prevent further downward movement. Resistance levels, on the other hand, are price levels where selling pressure is anticipated to prevent further upward movement. These levels are crucial for determining potential entry and exit points.

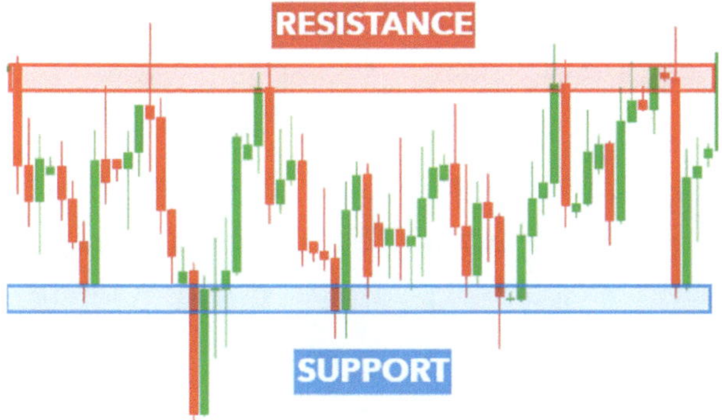

Example of support and resistance levels

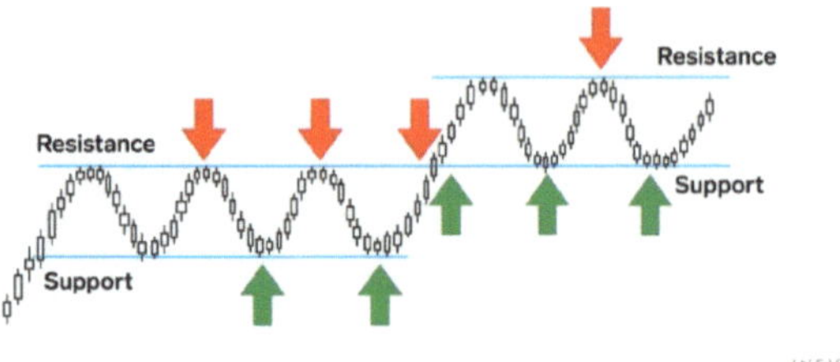

Technical Analysis and Fundamental Analysis

Fundamental analysis involves analyzing a company's financial statements to determine the fair value of the business, while technical analysis assumes that a security's price already reflects all publicly available information and instead focuses on the statistical analysis of price movements. Technical analysis attempts to understand the market sentiment behind price trends by looking for patterns and trends rather than analyzing a security's fundamental attributes.

Charles Dow released a series of editorials discussing technical analysis theory. His writings included basic assumptions that have continued to form the framework for technical analysis trading. Markets are efficient with values representing factors that influence a security's price, but even random market price movements appear to move in identifiable patterns and trends that tend to repeat themselves.

Technical analysts expect that prices, even in random market movements, will exhibit trends regardless of the time frame being observed. In other words, a stock price is more likely to continue a past trend than move erratically. Most technical trading strategies are based on this assumption.

Remember that technical analysts believe that history tends to repeat itself. The repetitive nature of price movements is often attributed to market psychology, which tends to be very predictable based on emotions like fear or excitement. Technical analysis uses chart patterns to analyze these emotions and subsequent market movements to understand trends. While many forms of technical analysis have been used for more than 100 years, they are still believed to be relevant because they illustrate patterns in price movements that often repeat themselves.

SECTION 11: Fundamental Analysis

Fundamental analysis and technical analysis are two different approaches used to analyze and make investment decisions in financial markets, Fundamental Analysis and Technical Analysis:

Technical Analysis:

Fundamental analysis is a method of evaluating the intrinsic value of an asset, such as stocks, bonds, or currencies, by examining the underlying factors that influence its value. It focuses on analyzing economic, financial, and qualitative factors to determine whether an asset is overvalued or undervalued.

Key elements of fundamental analysis include:

Company Financials: Evaluating financial statements, such as balance sheets, income statements, and cash flow statements, to assess the financial health and performance of a company.

Economic Factors: Examining macroeconomic indicators, such as Gross Domestic Product (GDP) growth, inflation rates, interest rates, and government policies, to gauge the overall economic conditions and their impact on the asset.

Industry Analysis: Assessing the competitive landscape, market dynamics, and industry trends to understand the potential growth prospects and risks associated with the asset.

Qualitative Factors: Considering non-financial aspects, such as management quality, brand reputation, market position, and regulatory environment, which can influence the asset's value.

Fundamental analysis aims to identify assets that are either undervalued or overvalued relative to their intrinsic worth. This information helps investors make decisions on buying, selling, or holding assets for the long term. Fundamental analysis is commonly used in stock valuation and is often favored by long-term investors and value-oriented traders.

Technical Analysis vs. Fundamental Analysis

Fundamental analysis and technical analysis, the major schools of thought when it comes to approaching the markets, are at opposite ends of the spectrum. Both methods are used for researching and forecasting future trends in stock prices, and like any investment strategy or philosophy, both have their advocates and adversaries. However, the two types of analysis differ.

Fundamental analysis is a method of evaluating securities by attempting to measure the intrinsic value of a stock. Fundamental analysts study everything from the overall economy and industry conditions to the financial condition and management of companies. Earnings, expenses, assets, and liabilities are all important characteristics to fundamental analysts.

Technical analysis differs from fundamental analysis in that the stock's price and volume are the only inputs. The core assumption is that all known fundamentals are factored into price; therefore, there is no need to pay close attention to them. Technical analysts do not attempt to measure a security's intrinsic value, but instead, use stock charts to identify patterns and trends that suggest what a stock will do in the future.

There are a variety of ways to learn technical analysis. The first step is to learn the basics of investing, stocks, markets, and financials. This can all be done through books, online courses, online material, and classes. Once the basics are understood, you can use the same types of materials but those that focus specifically on technical analysis. *Investopedia*'s course on technical analysis is one specific option.

SECTION 12: TradingView

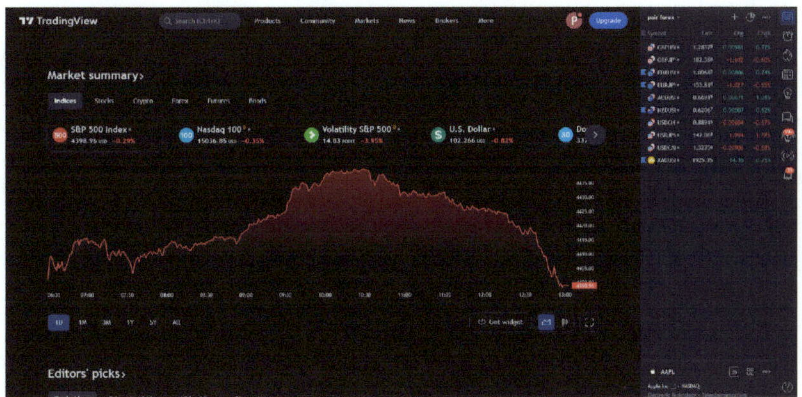

TradingView is a popular online platform that provides charting, analysis, and trading tools for various financial markets. It offers a wide range of features designed to assist traders and investors in making informed trading decisions. Here are some key aspects of TradingView:

Interactive Charts: TradingView offers interactive and customizable charts with a wide selection of technical indicators, drawing tools, and charting styles. Users can adjust the time frame, add multiple indicators, overlay various symbols, and annotate charts to conduct technical analysis.

Social Community: TradingView has a social component that allows users to share ideas, analysis, and trading strategies with the community. Traders can follow other users, join discussions, and engage in real-time chats to exchange insights and learn from others.

Trading Ideas and Scripts: Traders can publish their trading ideas, strategies, and scripts on TradingView. Users can browse and access a vast library of published trading ideas, indicator scripts, and trading algorithms created by other community members. This feature encourages collaboration and idea generation among traders.

Real-Time Data: TradingView provides real-time market data for various financial instruments, including stocks, cryptocurrencies, forex, and commodities. Users can access live price quotes, order books, and market depth information, depending on the data sources available.

Backtesting and Strategy Development: TradingView allows users to backtest trading strategies using historical data to assess their performance. Traders can develop and test their trading ideas by applying indicators, setting rules, and analyzing results using the built-in strategy tester.

Integration with Brokers: TradingView offers integration with several brokerage firms, allowing users to execute trades directly from the TradingView platform, provided they have an account with a supported broker.

Mobile Apps: TradingView provides mobile applications for iOS and Android devices, enabling users to access charts, analysis, and their trading ideas on the go.

TradingView offers both free and paid subscription plans. The free version provides basic features, while paid plans offer additional benefits such as more real-time data, advanced charting tools, and enhanced collaboration features.

Overall, TradingView has gained popularity among traders and investors due to its user-friendly interface, extensive charting capabilities, social community, and the ability to share and access trading ideas and strategies. It serves as a comprehensive platform for technical analysis and trading across various financial markets.

SECTION 13: Chart Patterns

An uptrend is an overall move (higher in price) created by higher highs and higher lows. It describes when the price is moving upward or getting higher. The uptrend is composed of higher swing lows and higher swing highs.

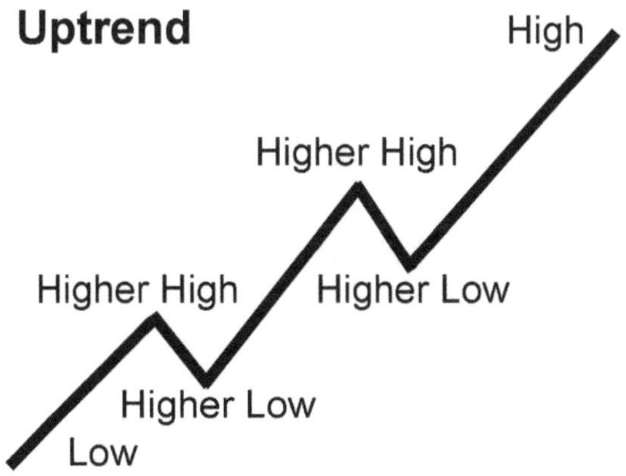

As long as the price is making these higher swing lows and higher swing highs, the uptrend is considered intact. Once the price starts making lower swing highs or lower swing lows, the uptrend is in question or has reversed into a downtrend.

When used in trading, "long" refers to a position that makes a profit if an asset's market price increases.

The term is usually used in context as "going long" or "taking a long position." When you trade in the forex market, since you buy or sell in currency pairs, "going long" means that you are buying the base currency and selling the quote currency. For example, if you go long on EUR/USD, you are buying euros and selling US dollars. Going long is the opposite of going short/shorting, which means taking a position that makes a profit if an asset's market price falls. Taking a long position doesn't necessarily mean buying an asset. Derivatives

allow traders to take a long position on a market without actually buying the underlying asset.

These are examples of an uptrend:

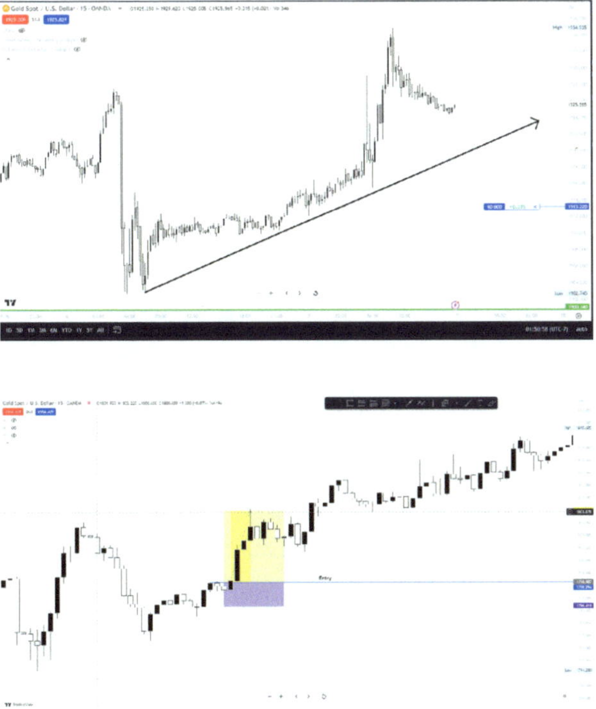

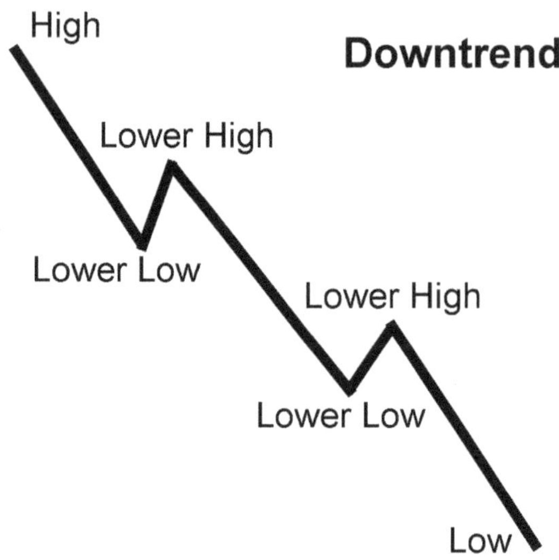

A downtrend is an overall move lower in price, created by lower lows and lower highs. A downtrend describes the price movement of a financial asset when the overall direction is downward. In a downtrend, each successive peak and trough is lower than the ones found earlier in the trend. The downtrend is therefore composed of lower swing lows and lower swing highs. As long as the price is making these lower swing lows and lower swing highs, the downtrend is considered intact.

These are examples of a downtrend:

ONCE THE PRICE STARTS MAKING HIGHER SWING HIGHS OR higher swing lows, the downtrend is in question or has reversed into an uptrend. This is also known as "short" or referred to as "going short."

MORE CHART PATTERNS

Double Top and Double Bottom are examples of chart patterns.

DOUBLE TOP

It is important to note that technical analysis is based on the premise that historical price data contains valuable information about future price movements. However, it has its limitations, and factors such as market sentiment, news events, and fundamental analysis can also impact prices. Traders often use a combination of technical and fundamental analysis to make informed trading decisions.

Double Bottom

Top-down analysis is an approach used in financial analysis and investing that involves examining the broader macroeconomic factors and market trends before focusing on specific individual investments. It starts with a macro-level analysis and gradually narrows down to a micro-level analysis.

SECTION 14: Supply and Demand vs Support and Resistance

Law of Supply and Demand
A theory that explains the interaction between the sellers of a resource and the buyers for that resource.

Demand

Supply

Supply and demand and support and resistance are two fundamental concepts in economics and financial markets. Any pricing in the forex market or any other market is determined by supply and demand.

The Law of Supply and Demand is essential because it helps investors, entrepreneurs, and economists understand and predict market conditions. For example, a company considering a price hike on a product will typically expect demand for it to decline as a result, and will attempt to estimate the price elasticity and substitution effect to determine whether to proceed regardless.

The degree to which changes in price translate into changes in demand and supply is known as the product's price elasticity. Demand for basic necessities is relatively inelastic, meaning it is less responsive to changes in price.

The same concept occurs in the financial markets. When a currency pair enters the selling zone, a level of friction occurs, and supply and demand trading begins. The sellers consider there is a better chance of selling at an inflated price. When pairs drop to a lower level and enter a demand zone, the opposite also takes place. In this instance, purchasers determine that buying the currency pair is more advantageous.

While supply and demand and support and resistance are related, they have distinct meanings and implications.

SUPPLY AND DEMAND:

The Law of Supply
The microeconomic law that states that, all other factors being equal, as the price of a good or service increases, the quantity of goods or services that suppliers offer will increase, and vice versa.

Law of Demand
A fundamental principle of economics that states that at a higher price consumers will demand a lower quantity of a good.

Every forex trader has a favorite strategy. Supply and demand is one of the most often utilized techniques. Supply and demand refers to the relationship between the quantity of a product or asset available (supply) and the desire or need for that product or asset (demand). In essence, it represents the interaction between buyers (demand) and sellers (supply) in a market.

The law of supply and demand states that as the price of a product or asset increases, the quantity supplied increases, while the quantity demanded decreases, and vice versa. When supply exceeds demand, prices tend to decrease, and when demand exceeds supply, prices tend to increase. The equilibrium point is where supply and demand are balanced, resulting in a stable price.

In financial markets, supply and demand dynamics impact the prices of assets, such as stocks, currencies, commodities, and bonds. If there is high demand for a particular asset and limited supply, the price is likely to increase. Inversely, if there is an oversupply and low demand, the price is likely to decrease.

The possibilities of a breakout rise as long as the price tests the same level. Support and resistance levels are undoubtedly levels to act on while we are in a trade, even though, in my opinion, they are not the best levels to trade. They are advantageous levels for rolling stop losses or for closing all or a portion of a position.

Support and resistance:

Support and resistance are terms used in technical analysis to describe price levels at which an asset tends to find buying support (support level) or selling pressure (resistance level).

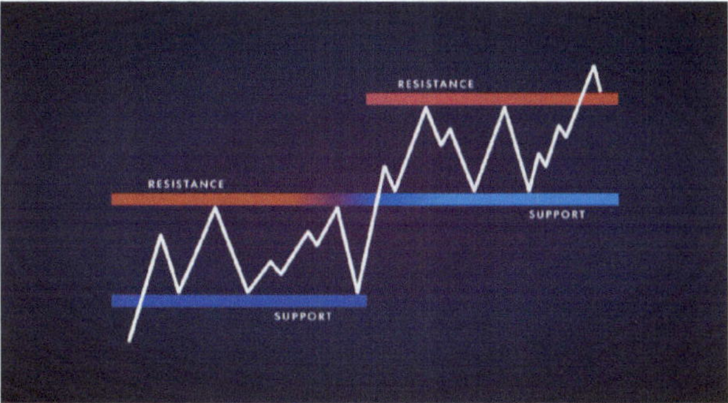

Support level: A support level is a price level where there is a significant number of buyers or demand for an asset. It acts as a floor or a price level that tends to prevent the asset's price from falling further. When the price approaches or touches the support level, buyers are more likely to enter the market and support the asset's price, causing it to bounce back or stabilize.

Resistance level: A resistance level is a price level where there is a significant number of sellers or supply of an asset. It acts as a ceiling or a price level that tends to prevent the asset's price from rising further. When the price approaches or reaches the resistance level, sellers are more likely to enter the market and sell the asset, creating selling pressure that can cause the price to reverse or consolidate.

Support and resistance levels are observed on price charts and are often identified based on previous price history, where the price has repeatedly bounced off or struggled to break through certain levels. Traders and investors use these levels to make decisions about entry and exit points. Support levels can be considered potential buying opportunities, while resistance levels can be seen as potential selling opportunities.

The red band on the following picture indicates a resistance zone, and the green band indicates a supply zone.

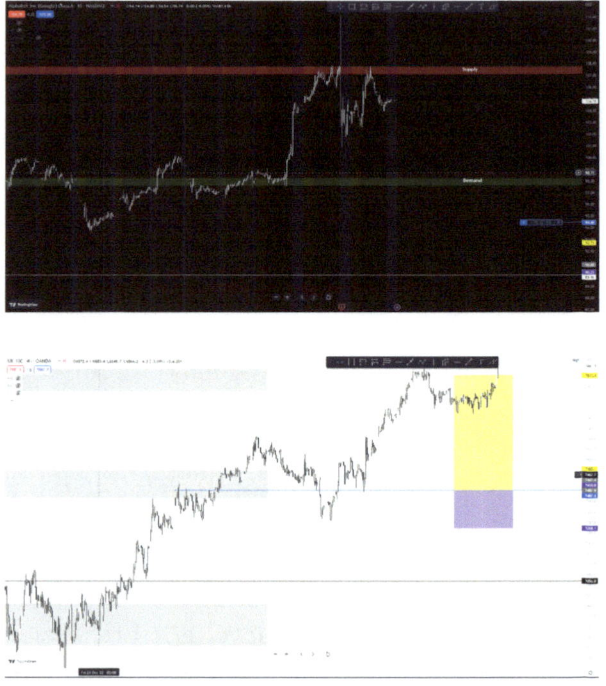

Institutional fund companies, the central banks, the public banks, etc., can all generate an enormous flood of orders. Individual traders typically lack the purchasing power necessary to make such large purchases and have such a significant impact on the market. Following the enormous buying/selling, an imbalance occurs.

An imbalance is a large number of unfulfilled orders at the supply or demand level that were submitted into the banking system. The price quickly deviates from the initial level. When the price returns to the target range, the major institutions then wait, hoping that their orders will be fulfilled.

The most professional and secure strategy to stay successful and achieve a fantastic risk-reward ratio is to start by only trading supply and demand. Supply and demand are generally the best levels to trade after they are generated because they are frequently the most crucial levels on the chart. There are a significant number of unfulfilled orders on these tiers. Trading support and resistance levels are riskier than trading supply and demand levels.

THE BENEFITS OF USING SUPPLY AND DEMAND IN Trading

The ability to take a vacation from the trading screen is a pleasant perk of supply and demand trading. This allows traders to establish and wait at predefined price levels. For traders who do not want to sit and watch every action on the screen, this is fantastic.

IN SUMMARY, SUPPLY AND DEMAND REFERS TO THE relationship between the quantity of a product or asset and the desire or need for that product or asset, influencing its price. Support and resistance, on the other hand, are specific price levels identified on charts, where an asset tends to find buying support or selling pressure, impacting its short-term price movements.

All supply and demand levels that serve as support and

resistance were initially points where a price had already been confirmed and checked a number of times in order to fulfill open orders. Supply or demand formed to support and resistance once the price was set on these levels a few times. In the end, supply turns into resistance while demand turns into support.

SECTION 15: Technical Indicators
(MACD, RSI, Fibonacci)

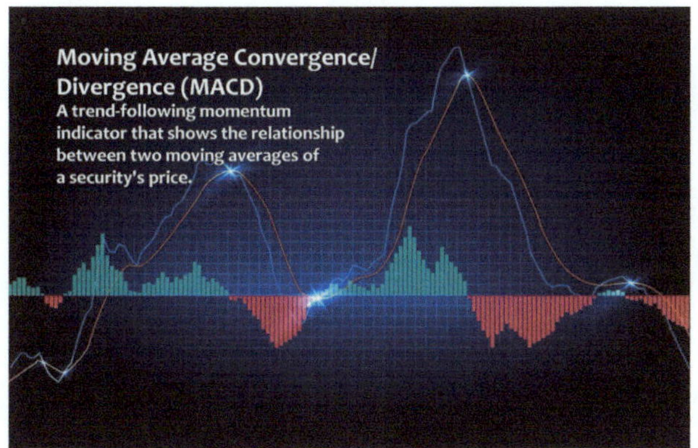

Technical indicators are mathematical calculations or statistical tools used in technical analysis to interpret and analyze historical market data. They help traders and investors identify potential trends, price reversals, overbought or oversold conditions, and other patterns that can assist in making trading decisions.

Two Types of Technical Indicators

Overlays: Technical indicators that use the same scale as prices are plotted over the top of the prices on a stock chart. Examples include moving averages and Bollinger Bands.

Oscillators: Technical indicators that oscillate between a local minimum and maximum are plotted above or below a price chart. Examples include the stochastic oscillator, MACD, or RSI.

Traders often use many different technical indicators when analyzing a security. With thousands of different options, traders must choose the indicators that work best for them and familiarize themselves with how they work. Traders may also combine technical indicators with more subjective forms of technical analysis, such as looking at chart patterns, to come up with trade ideas. Technical indicators can also be incorporated into automated trading systems, given their quantitative nature.

Here are explanations of commonly used technical indicators: Moving Average Convergence Divergence (MACD), Relative Strength Index (RSI), Fibonacci Retracement, and Moving Average.

Moving Average Convergence Divergence (MACD):

The MACD is a popular trend-following momentum indicator. It consists of two lines: the MACD line and the signal line. The MACD line is calculated by subtracting the 26-period exponential moving average (EMA) from the 12-

period EMA. The signal line is a 9-period EMA of the MACD line.

Traders use the MACD to identify potential buy and sell signals. When the MACD line crosses above the signal line, it generates a bullish signal, indicating that it may be a good time to buy. Inversely, when the MACD line crosses below the signal line, it generates a bearish signal, suggesting that it may be a good time to sell.

Relative Strength Index (RSI):

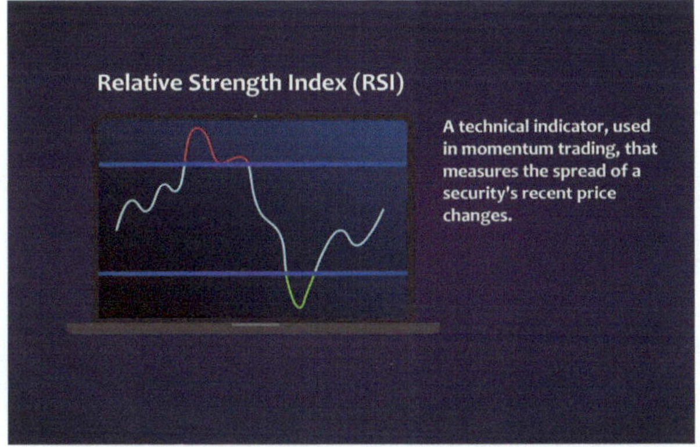

The RSI is a popular oscillator that measures the speed and change of price movements. It oscillates between 0 and 100. The RSI compares the magnitude of recent gains and losses over a specified period to determine whether an asset is overbought or oversold.

An RSI reading above 70 is typically considered overbought, indicating that the asset may be due for a price correction or reversal. Conversely, an RSI reading below 30 is considered oversold, suggesting that the asset may be undervalued and due for a potential price bounce.

Traders use the RSI to identify potential entry and exit points. For example, if the RSI is above 70 and starts to decline, it may signal a potential sell opportunity. Inversely, if the RSI is below 30 and starts to rise, it may indicate a potential buy opportunity.

Fibonacci Retracement:

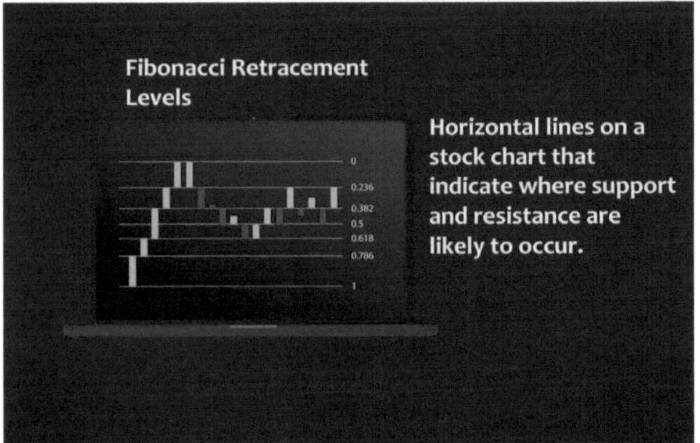

Fibonacci retracement levels are based on the Fibonacci sequence, a mathematical sequence where each number is the sum of the two preceding numbers (e.g., 0, 1, 1, 2, 3, 5, 8, 13, 21, etc.). In technical analysis, Fibonacci retracement is used to identify potential support and resistance levels based on these ratios.

Traders use Fibonacci retracement levels to identify potential areas of price retracement after a significant price move. The key Fibonacci retracement levels are 23.6%, 38.2%, 50%, 61.8%, and 78.6%. These levels are drawn from the high point to the low point (in a downtrend) or from the low point to the high point (in an uptrend) to identify potential levels where the price may bounce or reverse.

Moving Average:

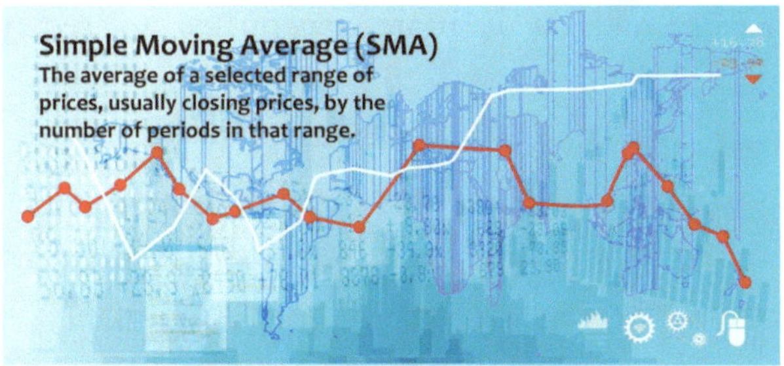

Moving averages are a widely used technical analysis tool that helps traders and investors smooth out price data and identify trends. A moving average is a calculation that provides an average value of a security's price over a specified period, continuously updating as new data points are added.

Here's how moving averages work:

Calculation: To calculate a moving average, you select a specific period (e.g., 10 days, 50 days, 200 days) and add up the closing prices of the security for that period. Then, you divide the sum by the number of periods chosen. This calculation is repeated for each subsequent period, shifting the calculation window forward.

Smoothing: Moving averages smooth out the price data by reducing short-term fluctuations and noise. By taking an average over a specific period, the impact of individual price movements is diluted, providing a clearer view of the underlying trend.

Trend Identification: Moving averages help identify trends in the price of a security. A simple moving average (SMA) provides an average value based on the closing prices, while an exponential moving average (EMA) places more weight on recent prices, making it more responsive to recent price changes.

Support and Resistance: Moving averages can act as support or resistance levels. For example, if the price of a security is trending upward and consistently finding support near a specific moving average, it suggests that the moving average is acting as a support level. Conversely, if the price consistently encounters resistance near a moving average during a downtrend, it can be considered a resistance level.

Crossovers: Moving averages can generate trading signals when different moving averages cross each other. For instance, a bullish signal occurs when a shorter-term moving average (e.g., 50-day SMA) crosses above a longer-term moving average (e.g., 200-day SMA). This crossover may indicate a potential upward trend and provide a buy signal. Conversely, a bearish signal occurs when a shorter-term moving average crosses below a longer-term moving average, indicating a potential downward trend and providing a sell signal.

Moving averages can be customized to fit an individual trader's preferences and trading strategy. Traders often use multiple moving averages of different time periods simultaneously to confirm trends and generate more reliable signals.

It's important to note that moving averages are lagging indicators because they are based on past prices. Therefore, they may not accurately predict future price movements or capture sudden market shifts. Traders often use moving averages in combination with other technical indicators and analysis techniques to make informed trading decisions.

Traders may use Fibonacci retracement levels in combination with other technical indicators to confirm potential entry or exit points or to set stop-loss orders.

It's important to note that technical indicators should not be used in isolation but rather in conjunction with other forms of technical analysis and consideration of fundamental factors. Traders often customize the parameters of these indicators based on their trading style, timeframes, and the specific assets they are analyzing.

SECTION 16: Selecting a Brokerage Firm

After considering all the factors I mentioned previously, you're now ready to decide on a broker and open an account. When choosing a trading broker, there are a few points to consider: Is the broker US-regulated? How much leverage does the broker offer its clients? What are the spreads and/or commissions?

What are the withdrawal procedures and timeframes? What are the instruments and or assets the broker actually offers?

Not all brokers offer all traded commodities or assets. For example, a broker I used for years, Oanda, only offers the ability to trade foreign exchange currencies to its clients. This is great if all you like to do is trade currencies. However, if you desire to trade assets like the US30 "Dow Jones Industrial Average 30," the NAS100, and/or the S&P 500, you will not be able to do so with Oanda. These instruments are not offered on the brokerage platform.

THERE ARE SEVERAL TOP US-REGULATED BROKERAGE trading firms that are well-known and widely used by traders. Here are some of them:

TD Ameritrade: TD Ameritrade, now part of Charles Schwab, is a popular brokerage firm known for its robust trading platforms, extensive research tools, and a wide range of investment products. It offers commission-free trading for stocks, ETFs, and options, along with access to mutual funds, futures, and forex trading.

Charles Schwab: Charles Schwab is one of the largest brokerage firms in the US. It provides a comprehensive suite of investment services, including online trading for stocks, options, ETFs, and mutual funds. Schwab offers competitive pricing, a user-friendly trading platform, and a wide range of educational resources for investors.

Fidelity Investments: Fidelity is a well-established brokerage firm that offers a range of investment options, including stocks, options, ETFs, mutual funds, bonds, and retirement accounts. It provides a user-friendly trading platform, extensive research and analysis tools, and a wide selection of educational resources.

ETRADE: ETRADE is a popular online brokerage firm known for its intuitive trading platform, powerful tools, and extensive educational resources. It offers commission-free trading for stocks, options, and ETFs, along with access to futures and forex trading. ETRADE also provides banking services, including checking and savings accounts.

Interactive Brokers: Interactive Brokers is a well-established brokerage firm known for its advanced trading platform, low-cost trades, and wide range of investment products. It offers access to a broad array of global markets, including stocks, options, futures, forex, and fixed income. Interactive Brokers caters to both individual traders and institutional clients.

Robinhood: Robinhood is a popular commission-free trading platform known for its user-friendly mobile app and accessibility. It offers commission-free trading for stocks, ETFs, options, and cryptocurrencies. Robinhood has gained popularity among new and younger investors for its ease of use and simplified trading experience.

It's always recommended to review their offerings and suitability for your individual trading requirements before making a decision. Consulting with a financial advisor or seeking guidance from reputable sources can also provide valuable insights when choosing a brokerage firm.

It's also important to conduct thorough research and consider your specific trading needs, fees, available trading platforms, research tools, customer support, and regulatory compliance when selecting a brokerage firm. These firms mentioned above are reputable and regulated.

Regulated brokers are subject to strict rules and regulations that aim to protect investors and ensure fair trading practices. They provide greater transparency, security, and accountability. This helps to ensure that your investments are adequately protected, and you have access to appropriate recourse in case of any issues or disputes.

Many unregulated US brokers offer excessive leverage to entice or appeal to most beginning traders to join. Most brokers require you to undergo a verification process. This includes submitting forms of identification and completing an application to submit for an account. Once these steps have been validated and satisfied, the next step is to fund your account.

Some brokers have a minimum deposit amount required. If the broker requires a minimum deposit amount, you have to use an exchange like Coinbase or Robinhood to transfer the money into the brokerage account if you're concerned with the fastest means of accessibility. You can also use your bank account to transfer funds, but this usually takes 3-5 days to clear before the funds can be available to trade. However, using a crypto exchange method is the easiest way I found to purchase the amount you like to deposit in Bitcoin. Simply transfer the funds from Bitcoin to the respective broker account. This is by far the fastest way to get immediate access to the funds to begin trading the market.

SECTION 17: Opening a Broker Account

Opening a broker account to trade typically involves the following steps:

Research and Compare Brokers: Start by researching and comparing different brokerage firms to find one that aligns with your trading needs. Consider factors such as trading fees, account types, available markets and instruments, trading platforms, customer support, and regulatory compliance. Read reviews and gather information to make an informed decision.

Choose an Account Type: Once you have selected a broker, determine the type of account that suits your trading preferences. Common account types include individual accounts, joint accounts, corporate accounts, retirement accounts, and margin accounts. Each account type may have specific requirements and features, so choose the one that best suits your needs.

Complete the Application: Visit the broker's website and locate the account opening section. Fill out the online application form, providing accurate personal information, contact details, and financial information as required. You may need to provide proof of identification, such as a passport or driver's license, and proof of address, such as a utility bill or bank statement.

Verification Process: To comply with regulatory requirements, brokers typically require applicants to undergo a verification process. This involves submitting the necessary identification and address verification documents. The broker will review and verify the information provided, which may take a few days to complete.

Fund Your Account: Once your account is approved, you will need to fund it to start trading. Most brokers offer various funding methods, such as bank transfers, credit/debit cards, or electronic payment systems. Choose the method that is convenient for you and follow the instructions provided by the broker to deposit funds into your trading account.

Select Trading Platform: Brokers often provide their own trading platforms or support popular third-party platforms. Familiarize yourself with the trading platform provided by your broker and ensure it meets your requirements. Download and install the platform if necessary, and log in using the credentials provided by the broker.

Read Terms and Conditions: Take the time to carefully read and understand the broker's terms and conditions, including their trading policies, fees and commissions, margin requirements, and any other relevant information. This will help you have a clear understanding of the rules and guidelines set by the broker.

Start Trading: Once your account is funded and the trading platform is set up, you can start trading. Before placing trades, familiarize yourself with the platform's features, order types, and risk management tools. Develop a trading plan and strategy, and always trade within your risk tolerance.

Opening a broker account involves financial risks, so it's essential to educate yourself about trading principles, risk management, and market dynamics before diving into trading activities. Consider seeking advice from financial professionals, and always trade responsibly.

SECTION 18: MetaTrader Platforms MT4 vs MT5

Symbol is the asset you're trading.

Ticket is the numerical assigned number to your trade by the broker.

Type is the position of your trade. "Buy" or "Sell!"

Volume is the lot size. Always remember:

.01= 10 cents aka "**Micro lot**"

.10= $1.00 dollar aka "**Mini lot**"

1.0= $10.00 dollars aka "**Standard lot**"

*This helps to commit to memory or write it down.

Price is the current value of the asset when you placed or executed the trade.

*This includes margin and/or spread

S/L is "Stop Loss" the specific value you'd like your trade to limit or stop your loss.

T/P is "Take Profit" the specific value you'd like the trade to stop after it's reached profit.

Time is the time you placed your trade or executed your position.

Price is the real-time price or value of the asset as it fluctuates.

This same information can be found on your ticket order as well.

MetaTrader 4 (MT4) and MetaTrader 5 (MT5) are popular and widely used trading platforms developed by MetaQuotes Software Corporation. Both platforms are designed for online trading in various financial markets, including forex, stocks, commodities, and derivatives. However, there are some differences between the two versions:

MetaTrader 4 (MT4):

MT4 is the older version of the MetaTrader platform and remains one of the most widely used trading platforms in the industry. Key features of MT4 include:

User-Friendly Interface: MT4 has a simple and intuitive

interface, making it accessible for beginners and experienced traders alike.

Charting and Technical Analysis: MT4 offers robust charting capabilities and a wide range of technical indicators for in-depth analysis.

Automated Trading: MT4 allows users to create and execute automated trading strategies using Expert Advisors (EAs), which are customizable trading algorithms.

Backtesting: Traders can test their strategies on historical data using the built-in backtesting functionality.

Market Access: MT4 provides access to a large number of brokers and liquidity providers, enabling traders to execute trades in various financial markets.

MetaTrader 5 (MT5):

MT5 is the successor to MT4 and offers additional features and enhanced capabilities compared to its predecessor. Key features of MT5 include:

Extended Asset Classes: MT5 allows trading not only in forex but also in other asset classes such as stocks, futures, and options.

Depth of Market: MT5 provides a depth-of-market feature, allowing traders to see the liquidity available at different price levels.

Improved Strategy Testing: MT5 offers enhanced backtesting capabilities with access to more historical data and more advanced testing options.

Economic Calendar: MT5 includes an integrated economic calendar, providing real-time financial news and events that can impact the markets.

Additional Order Types: MT5 offers additional order types, including stop-limit orders, which allow for more precise trade execution.

While MT5 offers additional features and asset classes, MT4 remains widely used due to its simplicity, extensive community support, and the availability of custom indicators and EAs developed specifically for the platform. The choice between MT4 and MT5 ultimately depends on an individual trader's needs, trading style, and the asset classes they wish to trade. Please keep in mind that these are downloadable platforms that are add-ons. You must link your specific broker to the platform when attempting to log in.

SECTION 19: Paper Trading

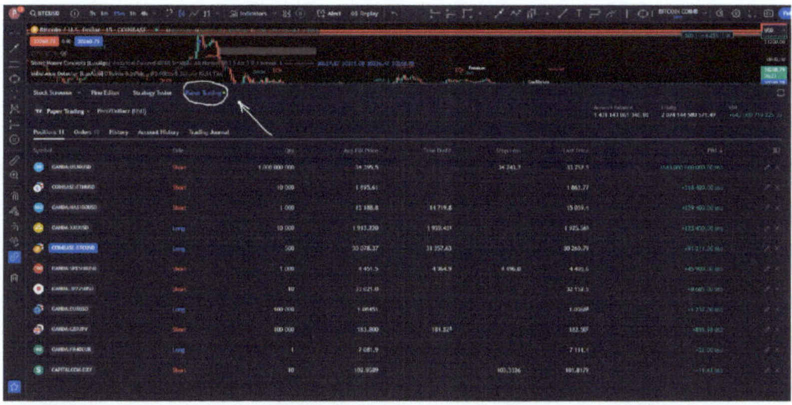

Paper trading, also known as virtual trading or simulated trading, is a practice in which traders and investors simulate trading activities without using real money. It involves using a trading platform or software to execute trades using virtual funds, typically with real-time market data.

Here are some key points about paper trading:

Simulated Environment: Paper trading creates a simulated trading environment that mirrors real market conditions. Traders can experience the process of placing trades, monitoring positions, and analyzing market movements without the risk of losing actual capital.

Virtual Funds: Paper trading accounts provide users with virtual funds or a simulated portfolio to trade with. These funds have no real-world value and are solely for practice purposes.

Real-Time Market Data: Paper trading platforms often provide access to real-time market data, allowing traders to observe and react to price movements as if they were trading with real money. This helps users understand how their strategies would have performed in real-time scenarios.

Learning and Skill Development: Paper trading is commonly used as a learning tool for traders to develop and refine their trading skills. It allows traders to experiment with different strategies, test new trading ideas, and gain experience without the risk of financial loss.

Risk-Free Environment: Since paper trading does not involve real money, traders can explore different trading techniques and take risks they might not be willing to take with their actual funds. It helps build confidence and familiarity with trading practices.

Performance Evaluation: Paper trading allows traders to evaluate the performance of their trading strategies without the emotional impact of real money. Traders can analyze their trades, assess their risk management, and identify areas for improvement.

Paper trading can be particularly useful for novice traders

who are new to the markets and want to gain practical experience before committing real funds. It can also benefit experienced traders who want to test new strategies or explore different markets without incurring financial risks.

However, it's important to note that paper trading has limitations. It cannot fully replicate the psychological and emotional aspects of trading with real money, which can significantly impact decision-making. Traders may experience different outcomes when transitioning from paper trading to live trading due to factors such as slippage, liquidity, and psychological factors.

Overall, paper trading serves as a valuable tool to practice and refine trading skills, test strategies, and gain confidence in trading without risking real capital.

Paper trading is important for several reasons:

Skill Development: Paper trading allows traders to practice and develop their trading skills in a risk-free environment. It provides an opportunity to learn how to place trades, monitor positions, and execute trading strategies without the fear of losing real money. By engaging in simulated trading, traders can gain experience and familiarity with the trading process, improve their decision-making abilities, and refine their trading techniques.

Strategy Testing: Paper trading allows traders to test and evaluate various trading strategies without risking actual capital. Traders can explore different approaches, analyze the performance of their strategies, and make adjustments as needed. It helps identify which strategies work well in specific market conditions and which ones may need refinement. Through repeated testing and iteration, traders can develop more effective and profitable trading strategies.

Risk Management: Proper risk management is crucial in trading. Paper trading enables traders to practice risk management techniques and assess the potential impact of different risk levels on their simulated portfolios. Traders can test various stop-loss and take-profit levels, position sizing strategies, and risk-reward ratios to understand how these factors affect their overall trading performance. This helps traders gain a deeper understanding of risk management principles and develop disciplined trading habits.

Market Familiarity: Paper trading allows traders to become familiar with different financial markets, trading instruments, and trading platforms. Traders can explore various asset classes, test their strategies in different market conditions, and learn how to navigate the trading platform's features and tools. This familiarity is essential before committing real funds to live trading, as it reduces the chances of making costly mistakes due to lack of knowledge or experience.

Confidence Building: Trading can be psychologically challenging, and emotions can impact decision-making. Paper trading helps build confidence by allowing traders to see the results of their trades and strategies in a controlled environment. As traders achieve consistent positive outcomes and gain confidence in their abilities, they are better prepared to handle the emotional aspects of live trading.

Learning from Mistakes: Paper trading provides an opportunity to make and learn from mistakes without financial consequences. Traders can analyze their trading decisions, evaluate the outcomes, and identify areas for improvement. This reflective process helps traders refine their strategies, avoid repeating past errors, and make more informed decisions in live trading.

Overall, paper trading is important because it offers a safe and controlled environment for traders to learn, practice, and refine their trading skills. It allows traders to gain experience, test strategies, develop risk management techniques, and build confidence before transitioning to live trading with real funds.

SECTION 20: Trade Entry / Trade Exits

In trading, a trade entry refers to the point at which traders initiate a new position in a financial instrument, such as buying a stock or opening a trade in the forex market based on their analysis and trading strategy.

There are various methods and factors that traders consider when determining the trade entry, including:

Technical Analysis: Traders may use technical indicators, chart patterns, trend lines, and other tools to identify potential entry points. For example, a trader might enter a long position when a stock's price breaks above a key resistance level or when a certain indicator generates a buy signal.

Fundamental Analysis: Traders who rely on fundamental analysis examine economic data, news events, company financials, and other factors to identify opportunities. They may enter a trade based on positive earnings reports, favorable economic indicators, or other fundamental catalysts.

Price Action: Price action traders analyze the movement of price itself to identify patterns, support and resistance levels, and other price-based signals that suggest an optimal entry point. They may enter a trade when they see a specific candlestick pattern, a breakout, or a reversal.

Risk Management: Traders also consider their risk tolerance and money management principles when determining the trade entry. They may set specific entry criteria based on their desired risk-reward ratio and position sizing rules.

On the other hand, a trade exit refers to the point at which traders close their existing position and exit the market. The trade exit is a critical decision that determines the outcome of the trade in terms of profit or loss. Traders use various methods to determine the trade exit, including:

Profit Target: Traders may set a predetermined profit target based on their desired return or a specific technical level. Once the price reaches the profit target, the traders exit the trade to lock in their gains.

Stop Loss: A stop loss is a predefined price level at which traders are willing to exit trades to limit their potential losses. It is used to protect against unfavorable price movements. If the price reaches the stop-loss level, the trade is automatically closed.

Trailing Stop: A trailing stop is a dynamic stop-loss order that adjusts as the price moves in favor of the trade. It allows the trader to protect profits while allowing for potential further gains. The trailing stop adjusts based on a predetermined distance or percentage from the highest reached price.

Exit Signals: Traders may use technical indicators or specific price patterns to generate exit signals. For example, a trader may exit a trade when a certain indicator generates a sell signal or when a bearish reversal pattern appears.

The trade exit is crucial for managing risk, preserving profits, and adhering to the trading plan. It ensures that traders have a disciplined approach to both winning and losing trades.

Both trade entry and trade exit points are determined by a trader's individual strategy, analysis techniques, risk management principles, and market conditions. It's important for traders to have a well-defined plan for both trade entry and exit to effectively manage trades and achieve trading objectives.

Section 21: Placing Trades

Ticket Orders: How to Place Your Trade Using a Ticket Order.

There are several ways you can execute or place a trade. The best way, in my opinion, is to use a ticket order.

Below are the quick-acting toggle Buy or Sell buttons that appear on your broker's chart display.

These are examples of ticket orders and the components that relate to a trade. The ticket orders are examples from TradingView (See SECTION 12).

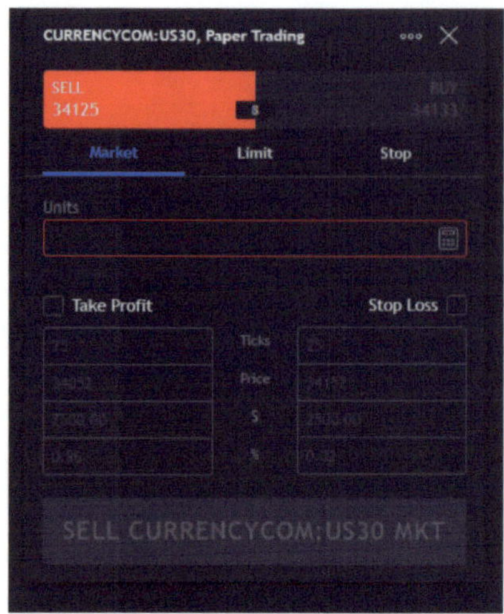

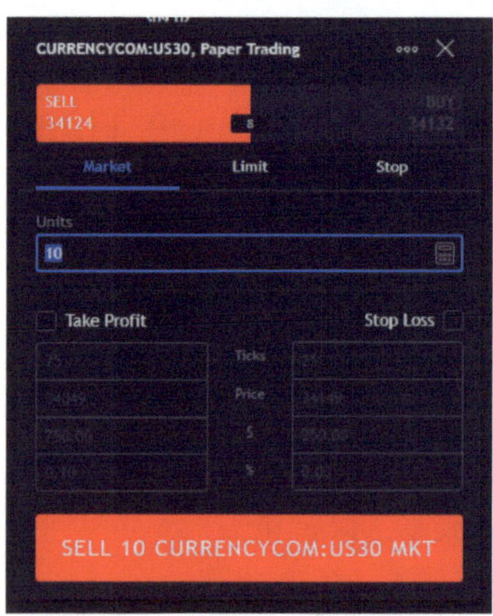

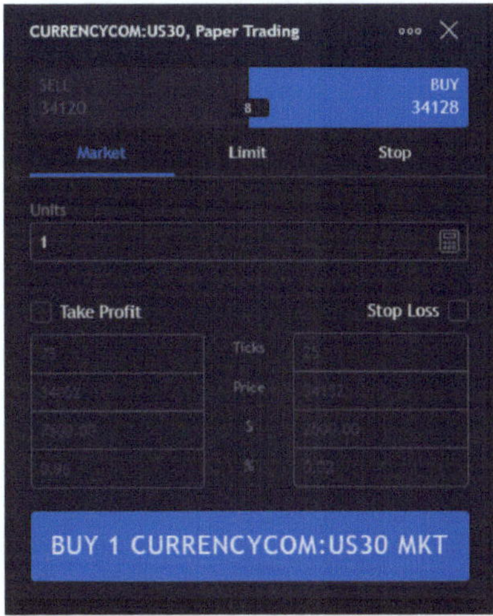

SECTION 22: Chart Time Frames

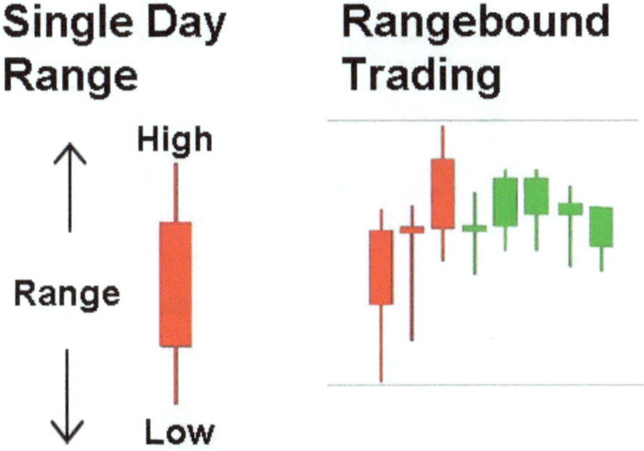

Chart time frame refers to the duration or interval used to display price data on a trading chart. In technical analysis, different time frames are used to analyze and interpret price patterns, trends, and other trading signals.

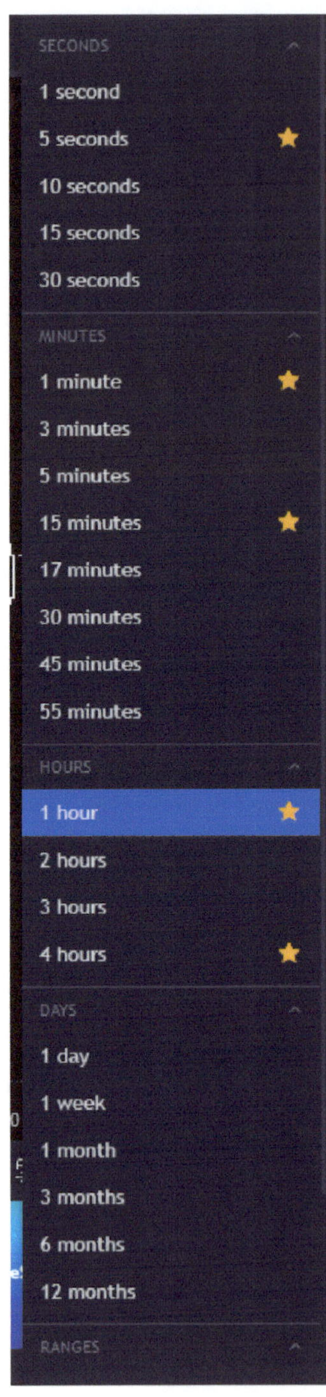
SECONDS
1 second
5 seconds
10 seconds
15 seconds
30 seconds
MINUTES
1 minute
3 minutes
5 minutes
15 minutes
17 minutes
30 minutes
45 minutes
55 minutes
HOURS
1 hour
2 hours
3 hours
4 hours
DAYS
1 day
1 week
1 month
3 months
6 months
12 months
RANGES

Trading charts can be displayed in various time frames, including:

Short-Term Time Frames: These time frames typically range from seconds to minutes and are commonly used by day traders and scalpers. Examples include 1-minute charts, 5-minute charts, and 15-minute charts. Short-term time frames provide a detailed view of price movements within a short period and are useful for identifying intraday trading opportunities.

Medium-Term Time Frames: These time frames range from hours to a few days. Examples include 1-hour charts, 4-hour charts, and daily charts. Medium-term time frames are commonly used by swing traders and position traders who hold trades for several days to weeks. They help identify trends and longer-term price patterns.

Long-Term Time Frames: These time frames can span weeks, months, or even years. Examples include weekly charts, monthly charts, and yearly charts. Long-term time frames are used by long-term investors and traders who take a broader view of the market. They help identify major trends, support and resistance levels, and significant price patterns.

The choice of chart time frame depends on the trader's trading style, goals, and time horizon. Short-term traders often focus on shorter time frames for quick trades, while longer-term traders and investors may prefer longer time frames for a more comprehensive analysis of price trends and patterns.

It is important to note that different time frames can produce different signals and interpretations. For example, a price pattern that appears significant on a daily chart may appear insignificant on a 15-minute chart. Traders often use multiple time frames to gain a more comprehensive understanding of the market dynamics and to confirm signals across different time horizons.

SECTION 23: Lot Size

The questions I get asked often are: "How much money should I start with?" or "How much money should I invest?" Well, these questions are very difficult to answer. I started off trading a total of $500, with a 10 cent, or .01, lot size. In using this method of trading, I became familiar with the term "lot size." The .01 meant I was trading .10 cent per pip. This is also known as a micro lot size. I know you are asking, "What is a pip?" To keep things simple, just know a pip is the Percentage In Point or Price Interest Point. It is the unit of measurement to express the change in value between two currencies.

The pip is calculated using the last decimal point. For example, in the currency pair EUR/USD, if the exchange rate goes from $1.11**68** to $1.11**69,** then you've earned 10 cents and went up 1 pip. The inverse is also true. If the exchange rate went from $1.11**68** to $1.11**67,** the price value went down 1 pip, and you would have lost 10 cents. A pip is usually the last decimal place of a price quote. The currency pair

USD/JPY is illustrated below. The second digit on the right of the decimal is the pip. Always pay close attention to your currency pairs and the amount of the lot size you wish to trade per pip.

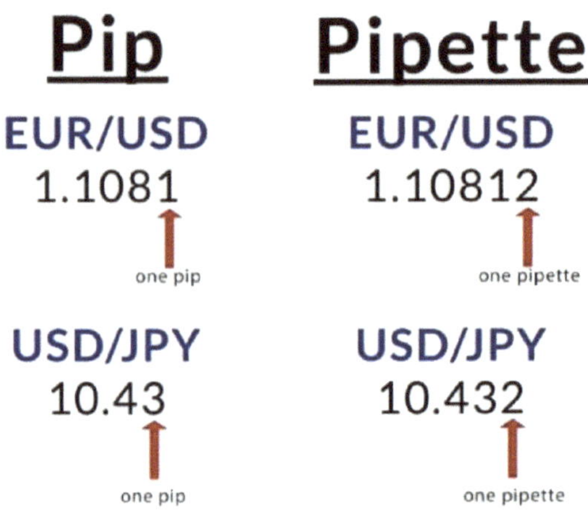

A tick and a pip are units of measurement used to quantify the price movements in financial markets. They are primarily used in trading and are especially relevant in forex and futures markets.

Tick: A tick represents the smallest possible price movement of an asset. It is the minimum increment by which the price can change. The tick size varies depending on the asset being traded and the exchange on which it is traded. For example, in the US stock market, the tick size for most stocks is one cent. So, if a stock is trading at $10.00 per share, the next tick up or down would be at $10.01 or $9.99, respectively.

Pip: Pip stands for "percentage in point" or "price interest point" and is primarily used in forex trading. It is a standardized unit of measurement for currency pairs. In most major currency pairs, such as EUR/USD or GBP/USD, a pip is typically equal to 0.0001 or 0.01% of the quoted price. However, for currency pairs involving the Japanese yen, a pip is usually equal to 0.01 or 0.01% of the quoted price due to the difference in decimal places.

For instance, if the EUR/USD currency pair is trading at 1.2500, and it moves up to 1.2501, it would represent a one-pip increase. Similarly, if the price moves down to 1.2499, it would be a one-pip decrease.

Pips are commonly used to calculate profits and losses in forex trading and to determine the spread (the difference between the buy and sell price) offered by brokers.

It's important to note that tick and pip sizes may vary depending on the specific asset, exchange, or trading platform being used. Traders should familiarize themselves with the tick and pip sizes relevant to their chosen markets and instruments.

A basis point (bps) or point, is a unit of measurement used to express small changes in percentage terms. It is equal to one-hundredth of a percentage point or 0.01%. Basis points are commonly used in finance to discuss interest rates, yields, and other financial metrics.

For example, let's consider an interest rate change from 2.50% to 2.75%. The difference between these two rates is 25 basis points. This means that the interest rate increased by 25 bps or 0.25%.

In the context of ticks, a tick refers to the minimum price movement of a financial instrument. The tick size varies depending on the asset being traded and the exchange on which it is traded. For example, in the US stock market, the tick size for most stocks is one cent. So, if a stock is trading at $10.00 per share and it moves up to $10.01, it would be a one-tick increase.

In summary, basis points and ticks are units of measurement used to quantify small changes in percentage terms and price movements, respectively. While basis points are typically used to discuss interest rates and yields, ticks are relevant in price movements of financial instruments.

SECTION 24: Spreads

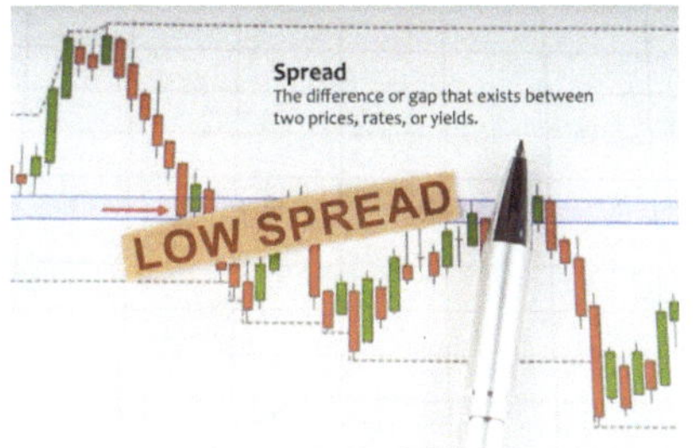

In the context of financial markets, spreads refer to the difference between the buy (bid) and sell (ask) prices of a financial instrument. It represents the cost or commission charged by brokers for executing trades. Spreads can be expressed in terms of pips, points, or as a percentage of the asset's price.

HERE ARE A FEW KEY POINTS ABOUT SPREADS:

Bid and Ask Prices: When trading, there are two primary prices associated with an asset—the bid price and the ask price. The bid price represents the highest price a buyer is willing to pay for the asset, while the ask price represents the lowest price a seller is willing to accept. The difference between these two prices is the spread.

Types of Spreads: There are two main types of spreads:

Fixed Spreads: Some brokers offer fixed spreads, which means the spread remains constant regardless of market conditions. This can be advantageous for traders as it provides certainty in terms of trading costs.

Variable Spreads: Variable spreads, also known as floating spreads, can change depending on market volatility and liquidity. When market conditions are more volatile, spreads tend to widen, while they narrow during times of lower volatility. Variable spreads are commonly found in forex trading and some other markets.

Other Information Regarding Spread:

Spread Size: The size of the spread can vary between different financial instruments and brokers. Highly liquid assets, such as major currency pairs, often have tighter spreads because they have high trading volume and greater liquidity. Less liquid assets or those with lower trading volume may have wider spreads.

Spread Costs: Spreads represent a cost to traders. When entering a trade, traders typically pay the spread as part of the transaction. For example, if the bid price for a stock is $10 and the ask price is $10.05, the spread is $0.05. This means a trader buying the stock would pay $10.05, while if they were to sell it immediately, they would receive $10. The difference between the buy and sell prices represents the cost of the spread.

Impact on Trading Costs: Spreads directly impact the profitability of trades. For short-term traders or scalpers who aim to capture small price movements, tighter spreads are generally more favorable as they reduce the cost of entering and exiting positions. Conversely, for longer-term traders, wider spreads may have a lesser impact on overall profitability.

Market Volatility: Spreads can fluctuate based on market conditions and volatility. During periods of high market volatility, spreads may widen as liquidity providers adjust their prices to reflect the increased uncertainty and risk.

Understanding spreads is crucial for traders because it impacts the cost of trading and potential profits. Traders should consider the spread offered by their chosen broker and evaluate its impact on their trading strategy and profitability.

SECTION 25: Leverage

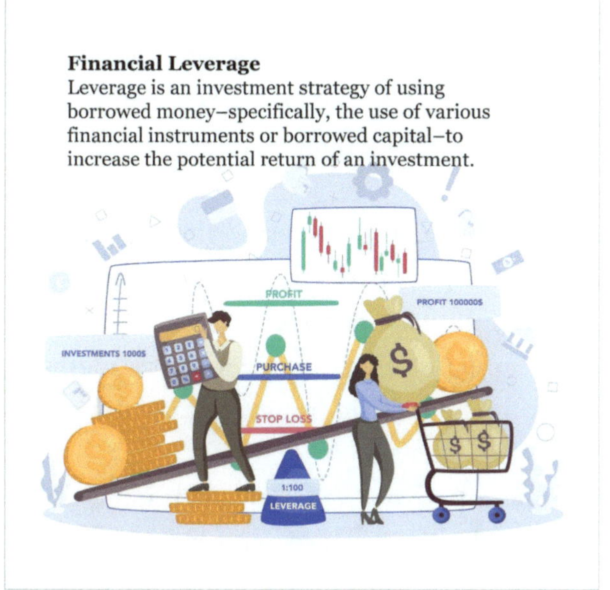

Trading leverage refers to the use of borrowed funds or financial instruments to increase the potential return on an investment. It allows traders to control larger positions in the market with a smaller initial investment, amplifying both potential profits and losses. Trading leverage is commonly used in various financial markets, including stocks, bonds, commodities, and foreign exchange.

When traders utilize leverage, they are essentially borrowing funds from a broker or financial institution to increase their trading position. The borrowed funds act as a multiplier, allowing the traders to control a larger position than they would with their own capital alone. The amount of leverage available to traders can vary depending on the financial market and the broker or platform being used.

Leverage is typically represented as a ratio or a percentage, indicating the amount of borrowed funds relative to traders' own capital. For example, a leverage ratio of 1:100 means that for every dollar of a trader's own capital, he/she can control $100 in the market. The specific leverage ratio available may depend on the broker's margin requirements and regulatory restrictions.

Trading leverage can be accessed through different financial instruments and methods, including margin trading, options trading, futures contracts, contracts for difference (CFDs), and forex trading. Each of these methods allows traders to amplify their positions and potentially increase their profits.

It is important to note that while trading leverage can magnify potential gains, it also increases the risk of losses. Traders who utilize leverage must be mindful of the potential downside and carefully manage their risk exposure. The use of leverage requires a thorough understanding of the financial markets, risk management strategies, and disciplined trading practices.

Overall, trading leverage offers traders the opportunity to access larger positions in the market and potentially increase their returns. However, it is essential for traders to approach leverage with caution, implement risk management techniques, and understand the potential risks involved in order to make informed trading decisions.

Types of trading:

Margin Trading: Margin trading is a popular method of trading with leverage in the stock market. Let's say you have $10,000 in your brokerage account and want to buy shares of a company. With a 2:1 leverage ratio, you can borrow an additional $10,000 from your broker, giving you a total purchasing power of $20,000. This allows you to control a larger position in the market and potentially increase your returns. However, it's important to note that losses are also magnified, so careful risk management is crucial.

Forex Trading: In the forex market, traders often utilize leverage to take advantage of small price movements in currency pairs. For instance, a leverage ratio of 1:100 means that for every $1 of your own capital, you can control $100 in the forex market. With leverage, even small fluctuations in exchange rates can result in significant profits or losses. It is essential to use appropriate risk management techniques and have a solid understanding of the forex market before trading with leverage.

Options Trading: Options trading provides an opportunity to trade with leverage. Options contracts give traders the right to buy (call option) or sell (put option) an underlying asset at a predetermined price within a specified timeframe. By purchasing options contracts, traders can control a larger position in the underlying asset than the initial investment would allow. This leverage amplifies potential gains but also increases the risk of losses.

Futures Trading: Futures contracts are agreements to buy or sell an asset at a predetermined price and date in the future. Futures trading allows traders to control a larger position in the underlying asset with a relatively small initial investment. For example, if the margin requirement for a futures contract is 10%, a trader with $10,000 could control a futures contract worth $100,000. This leverage enables traders to profit from price movements in the underlying asset.

SECTION 26: Contract for Difference (CFD)

Contract for Difference (CFD) Trading: CFDs are derivative instruments that allow traders to speculate on the price movements of various financial assets without owning the underlying asset. CFD trading often involves significant leverage, enabling traders to control larger positions. For example, a CFD broker might offer leverage of 1:50, meaning that for every $1 of your own capital, you can trade with $50 in the market. This allows traders to access a broader range of markets and potentially increase their returns.

It's important to note that while leverage can enhance potential profits, it also magnifies potential losses. Traders must have a thorough understanding of the risks involved and implement proper risk management techniques when trading with leverage.

SECTION 27: Margin

Margin
The collateral that an investor has to deposit with their broker or exchange to cover the credit risk the holder poses for the broker or the exchange.

Margin refers to the borrowed funds that traders and investors use to finance their investment positions. It allows individuals to trade with a larger capital than what they currently possess, leveraging their potential returns (or losses). Margin trading involves borrowing money from a broker or an exchange to buy or sell financial instruments, such as stocks, futures contracts, or currencies.

When engaging in margin trading, investors are required to deposit a certain amount of their own funds, known as the initial margin or margin requirement. The initial margin is typically a percentage of the total value of the investment position. The remaining funds are provided by the broker or exchange as a loan, referred to as the margin loan.

The concept of margin is also closely related to the concept of leverage. Leverage is the ratio between the total value of the investment position and the margin deposit. For example, if investors want to trade with a leverage of 1:5, they would need to deposit 20% of the total value of the position as margin, while the remaining 80% would be borrowed funds.

SECTION 28: Margin Call

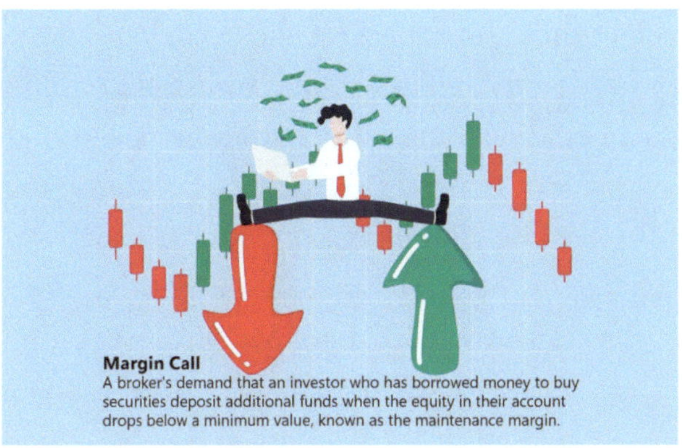

Margin accounts are subject to margin calls. A margin call occurs when the value of the investment position declines to a certain threshold, known as the maintenance margin level. At this point, the broker or exchange requires the investor to deposit additional funds to bring the margin back up to the initial margin level. Failure to meet a margin call may result in the broker liquidating the position to recover the borrowed funds.

Margin trading can amplify both profits and losses. While it offers the potential for higher returns, it also increases the risk of significant losses. Traders should exercise caution and carefully manage their margin positions to avoid excessive risk.

It's important to note that margin requirements, regulations, and available leverage may vary across different financial markets and jurisdictions. Traders should familiarize themselves with the specific margin rules and risks associated with the instruments they intend to trade before engaging in margin trading.

Margin and leverage are related concepts in trading, but they represent different aspects of the trading process:

Margin: Margin refers to the funds that traders must deposit to open and maintain a trading position. It is the investor's own capital that is used as collateral or a down payment for a trade. The margin amount is usually expressed as a percentage of the total value of the position and is determined by the broker or exchange. Margin serves as a form of security or guarantee for the borrowed funds.

For example, if an investor wants to buy $10,000 worth of stocks on margin and the broker has a margin requirement of 50%, the investor would need to deposit $5,000 as margin. The remaining $5,000 would be provided as a loan by the broker.

Leverage: Leverage refers to the ratio of the total value of the trading position to the margin deposit. It allows traders to control larger positions with a smaller amount of capital. Leverage is expressed as a ratio, such as 1:10, 1:50, or 1:100, indicating the multiple by which the position is magnified.

Continuing with the previous example, if the leverage offered by the broker is 1:2, the trader's $5,000 margin deposit would allow control of a position worth $10,000. This means that for every $1 of the trader's own capital, the trader has $2 of exposure in the market.

In summary, margin represents the actual funds deposited by the trader, while leverage determines the multiplier effect on the trading position. Margin is the trader's contribution to the trade, while leverage is the borrowing power provided by the broker or exchange. Higher leverage amplifies both potential profits and losses, increasing the risk involved in trading.

Margin and leverage requirements, as well as the associated risks, can vary depending on the financial instrument, trading platform, and regulatory guidelines. Traders should carefully consider their risk tolerance and understand the implications of trading on margin with leverage before entering into any positions.

SECTION 29: Glossary

Asset*:* An asset is a resource that has economic value and is owned or controlled by an individual, company, or organization. It represents something of value that can be used, sold, or exchanged to generate future income, provide benefits, or contribute to the wealth of the owner.

Alpha: Alpha is a measure of an investment's performance relative to a benchmark index. It represents the excess return that an investment generates above or below the benchmark. Positive alpha indicates outperformance, while negative alpha indicates underperformance.

Arbitrage: Arbitrage refers to the practice of exploiting price discrepancies in different markets or instruments to make a risk-free profit. Arbitrageurs buy an asset at a lower price in one market and sell it at a higher price in another market, taking advantage of temporary price inefficiencies.

Ask: The ask (or offer) represents the lowest price at

which a seller is willing to sell a financial instrument in a trading market. It is the price at which you can buy the asset.

Balance of Trade: Balance of trade refers to the difference between the value of a country's exports and the value of its imports over a specific period. A positive balance of trade (trade surplus) occurs when exports exceed imports, while a negative balance of trade (trade deficit) occurs when imports exceed exports.

Bear Market: A bear market is a financial market characterized by falling prices and a negative sentiment among investors. It typically signifies a prolonged period of declining prices and a pessimistic outlook for the market as a whole.

Bid: The bid represents the highest price at which a buyer is willing to purchase a financial instrument, such as a stock or currency pair, in a trading market.

Bid-Ask Spread: The bid-ask spread is the difference between the highest price a buyer is willing to pay (bid) and the lowest price a seller is willing to accept (ask) for a financial instrument. It represents the transaction cost or the commission charged by the broker for executing trades.

Beta: Beta is a measure of a stock's volatility or sensitivity to market movements. It compares the price movement of an individual stock to the price movement of a benchmark index. A beta greater than 1 indicates the stock is more volatile than the market, while a beta less than 1 indicates lower volatility.

Bollinger Bands: Bollinger Bands are a technical analysis tool used to measure price volatility and identify potential price reversals. They consist of a middle band (usually a moving average) and two outer bands that are standard deviations away from the middle band. The bands expand during periods of high volatility and contract during periods of low volatility.

Breakout: A breakout occurs when the price of a financial instrument moves above a significant resistance level or below a significant support level. It indicates a potential shift in the trend and often leads to increased momentum in the direction of the breakout.

Breakout Level: The breakout level is the specific price level at which a breakout occurs. It is the point at which the price surpasses a significant resistance or support level, triggering increased buying or selling pressure.

Bull Market: A bull market is a financial market characterized by rising prices and a generally positive sentiment among investors. It typically signifies an upward trend in prices over an extended period, accompanied by optimism and confidence in the market.

Bullish: Bullish refers to a positive or optimistic outlook for a particular financial instrument or market. It indicates a belief that prices will rise or that the market will experience upward momentum.

Candlestick: A candlestick is a graphical representation of price movements for a specific time period on a price chart. It consists of a rectangular "body" and "wicks" (or "shadows") that extend from the top and bottom of the body, indicating the price range between the high and low during that period.

Candlestick Pattern: Candlestick patterns are specific formations or combinations of candlesticks on a price chart. They are used in technical analysis to identify potential trend reversals, continuations, or patterns that may suggest future price movements.

Central Bank: A central bank is a financial institution responsible for managing a country's money supply, monetary policy, and interest rates. It acts as the banker to the government, regulates the banking system, and often serves as a lender of last resort.

Chart: A chart is a graphical representation of historical price data of a financial instrument. It displays the price movements over a specific time period and helps traders analyze trends, patterns, and potential trading opportunities.

Circuit Breaker: A circuit breaker is a mechanism used by stock exchanges to temporarily halt or suspend trading in response to significant market declines or volatility. It provides an opportunity for market participants to reassess and helps prevent excessive panic-selling or extreme price movements.

CPI (Consumer Price Index): The Consumer Price Index is a measure of inflation that tracks the average change in prices of a basket of goods and services consumed by households. It is used to gauge changes in the cost of living over time.

Contract for Difference (CFD): A Contract for Difference is a derivative product that allows traders to speculate on the price movements of financial instruments without owning the underlying asset. CFDs enable traders to take both long and short positions and can be used for various markets, including stocks, indices, commodities, and currencies.

Cup and Handle: Cup and handle is a bullish chart pattern that resembles a cup with a handle. It signifies a period of consolidation and potential continuation of an upward trend. Traders often see this pattern as a signal to enter long positions.

Dark Pool: A dark pool is a private or alternative trading venue where large institutional traders can anonymously trade large blocks of securities. Dark pools provide liquidity outside of the public exchange markets and allow for hidden order execution.

Day Order: A day order is an order to buy or sell a financial instrument that is valid only for the trading day it is placed. If the order is not executed by the end of the trading day, it is automatically canceled.

Day Trading: Day trading refers to the practice of buying and selling financial instruments within the same trading day. Day traders aim to profit from short-term price fluctuations and close their positions before the market closes.

Derivative: A derivative is a financial instrument whose value is derived from an underlying asset. Common types of derivatives include options, futures, swaps, and contracts for difference (CFDs).

Divergence: Divergence refers to a situation where the price of a financial instrument moves in the opposite direction of a technical indicator or another related asset. It can indicate a potential change in the trend or momentum of the instrument.

Dividend: A dividend is a payment made by a company to its shareholders as a distribution of profits. It is usually paid on a per-share basis and represents a portion of the company's earnings.

Double Top/Bottom: A double top is a chart pattern

that occurs when the price of a financial instrument reaches a high level, pulls back, and then rallies again to a similar high before reversing its trend. A double bottom is the inverse, with two significant lows followed by a rally. These patterns are often seen as potential trend-reversal signals.

Drawdown: Drawdown refers to the peak-to-trough decline in the value of an investment or trading account during a specific period. It measures the extent of loss experienced by an investor or trader before a recovery in value occurs.

Earnings: Earnings refer to the profits generated by a company during a specific period, typically reported quarterly or annually. Earnings are a key measure of a company's financial performance and are often used to assess its profitability and growth potential.

Economic Indicators: Economic indicators are statistical data points that provide insights into the overall health and performance of an economy. They include measures such as GDP (Gross Domestic Product), CPI (Consumer Price Index), unemployment rate, retail sales, and manufacturing activity. Economic indicators help analysts and investors assess the economic conditions and make informed decisions.

EPS (Earnings Per Share): Earnings Per Share (EPS) is a financial metric that represents the portion of a company's profit allocated to each outstanding share of its common stock. It is calculated by dividing the company's net earnings by the number of shares outstanding. EPS is widely used by investors to evaluate a company's profitability on a per-share basis.

ETF (Exchange-Traded Fund): An Exchange-Traded Fund (ETF) is a type of investment fund that trades on stock exchanges like a stock. It holds a diversified portfolio of assets, such as stocks, bonds, or commodities, and aims to track the performance of a specific index or sector. ETFs provide investors with the ability to gain exposure to a broad market or specific asset class in a convenient and cost-effective manner.

Execution: Execution refers to the process of carrying out a trade order and completing the transaction in the market. It involves matching the buy and sell orders at the specified price and quantity, resulting in the actual trade taking place.

Fiat Currency: Fiat currency is a type of currency that is issued by a government and declared to be legal tender for transactions within its jurisdiction. Unlike commodity money, which is backed by a physical commodity like gold or silver, fiat currency has no intrinsic value. Instead, its value is derived from the trust and confidence that people have in the government that issues it.

Fibonacci Extension: Fibonacci extension is a technical analysis tool that is used to identify potential price targets or levels of support and resistance beyond the current price range. It uses Fibonacci ratios, derived from a mathematical sequence, to project future price levels based on the price swings of a financial instrument.

Fibonacci Retracement: Fibonacci retracement is a technical analysis tool used to identify potential levels of support and resistance within a price trend. It uses Fibonacci ratios, derived from a mathematical sequence, to identify potential retracement levels based on the price swings of a financial instrument.

Fill: Fill refers to the execution of a trade order, where the order is matched with a counterparty and completed at the specified price. A fill occurs when the transaction is successfully executed and recorded.

Fill or Kill: Fill or Kill is a type of order instruction given to a broker or a trading platform. It requires the immediate execution of the entire order quantity at the specified price or better. If the order cannot be filled in its entirety, it is canceled.

Financial Analysis: Financial analysis involves evaluating the financial statements and performance of a company to assess its financial health, profitability, and investment potential. It includes analyzing financial ratios, cash flow, income statements, balance sheets, and other financial metrics.

Fiscal Policy: Fiscal policy refers to the use of government spending, taxation, and borrowing to influence the overall economy. It is used to manage economic growth, stabilize inflation, and address unemployment through adjustments in government spending and taxation levels.

FOMC (Federal Open Market Committee): The Federal Open Market Committee is the monetary policymaking body of the United States Federal Reserve. It is responsible for setting the nation's monetary policy, including decisions on interest rates, money supply, and economic stimulus measures.

Fundamental Analysis: Fundamental analysis is a method of evaluating securities or financial instruments by examining the underlying factors that can influence their value. It involves analyzing financial statements, economic indicators, industry trends, management quality, and other relevant information to assess the intrinsic value of an asset.

Futures: Futures are derivative financial contracts that obligate the buyer to purchase an underlying asset or the seller to sell an underlying asset at a predetermined price and date in the future. Futures are commonly used for speculative trading, hedging, and risk management purposes.

Good 'til Canceled (GTC): Good 'til Canceled is an instruction given to a broker or a trading platform to keep an order active until it is either executed, canceled by the trader, or a specified expiration date is reached. GTC orders remain in effect beyond the current trading session.

GDP (Gross Domestic Product): Gross Domestic Product is a measure of the total value of all goods and services produced within a country's borders over a specific period. It is used as an indicator of the economic health and size of a country's economy.

Head and Shoulders Pattern: The Head and Shoulders pattern is a technical chart pattern that indicates a potential trend reversal. It consists of three peaks, with the middle peak (the head) being higher than the two surrounding peaks (the shoulders). This pattern is considered bearish and suggests that a bullish trend may be ending.

Hedging: Hedging refers to a risk management strategy in which an investor or trader takes a position to offset potential losses in another investment. It involves opening a position that serves as a safeguard against adverse price movements or market conditions.

High-Frequency Trading (HFT): High-Frequency Trading is a trading strategy that uses advanced technology and algorithms to execute a large number of trades within extremely short time frames. HFT relies on the speed of execution to take advantage of small price discrepancies and market inefficiencies.

Higher High: In trading and technical analysis, a "higher high" refers to a specific pattern in price movement that occurs when the highest price of an asset during a particular time period is greater than the highest price reached during the previous time period. It is a key concept in analyzing price charts and identifying trends, especially in the context of uptrends.

Higher Low: In trading and technical analysis, a "higher low" is a term used to describe a pattern in price movement where the lowest point of a price retracement or correction during a specific time period is higher than the lowest point in the previous price retracement or correction. It's an essential concept for understanding trends and their potential continuations, particularly in the context of uptrends.

Ichimoku Cloud: The Ichimoku Cloud is a technical analysis tool that provides insights into potential support, resistance, and trend direction. It consists of several components, including a cloud or "kumo," which represents an area of potential support or resistance. Traders use the Ichimoku Cloud to identify trend reversals and gauge market momentum.

Imbalance: Imbalance refers to a situation where there is an unequal distribution between supply and demand for a particular financial asset or security.

Initial Margin: Initial Margin is the initial deposit required by a broker from a trader or investor when opening a leveraged position. It represents a percentage of the total value of the position and serves as collateral to cover potential losses.

Interest Rate: Interest Rate is the percentage charged by a lender to a borrower for the use of borrowed funds. It is typically expressed as an annual percentage rate and influences the cost of borrowing and the returns on savings and investments.

IPO (Initial Public Offering): Initial Public Offering is the process by which a private company offers its shares to the public for the first time, allowing it to be traded on a stock exchange. An IPO provides the company with access to capital and allows investors to purchase shares and become partial owners of the company.

Leverage: Leverage refers to using borrowed funds, such as margin, to increase the potential returns (and risks) of an investment. It allows traders and investors to control larger positions with a smaller amount of invested capital.

Limit Down: Limit Down refers to the maximum downward price movement allowed for a particular financial instrument within a trading session. It is a circuit breaker mechanism that halts trading or imposes restrictions when prices decline significantly.

Limit Order: A Limit Order is an order to buy or sell a financial instrument at a specified price or better. It is executed only at the specified price or more favorable. Limit orders are used to control the price at which a trade is executed.

Limit Up: Limit Up refers to the maximum upward price movement allowed for a particular financial instrument within a trading session. Similar to limit down, it acts as a circuit breaker to restrict trading when prices rise significantly.

Liquidity: Liquidity refers to the ease with which a financial instrument can be bought or sold in the market without significantly impacting its price. High liquidity means there are many buyers and sellers, resulting in tight bid-ask spreads and efficient trade execution.

Liquidity Pool: A Liquidity Pool is a reserve of funds or assets set aside to provide liquidity to a specific market or trading platform. Liquidity pools aggregate orders from multiple participants, enhancing liquidity and facilitating efficient trading.

Liquidity Provider: A Liquidity Provider is an entity, often a financial institution, that offers liquidity by providing continuous buy and sell quotes for financial instruments. Liquidity providers play a crucial role in maintaining market liquidity and ensuring smooth trade execution.

MACD (Moving Average Convergence Divergence): Moving Average Convergence Divergence is a popular technical analysis indicator that measures the relationship between two moving averages of a financial instrument's price. It helps identify potential trend reversals, momentum, and divergence between price and the indicator.

Maintenance Margin: Maintenance Margin is the minimum account balance required by a broker to keep a leveraged position open. It is set to ensure that the account has sufficient funds to cover potential losses and avoid a margin call.

Margin: Margin refers to the borrowed funds provided by a broker to a trader or investor for the purpose of trading larger positions than the trader's account balance would allow. It allows traders to leverage their capital and potentially amplify both profits and losses.

Margin Call: A Margin Call is a notification from a

broker to a trader or investor requesting additional funds or collateral when the account's margin falls below a specified level. It is triggered when losses on open positions exceed available account equity.

Market Depth: Market Depth refers to the display of buy and sell orders for a financial instrument at different price levels. It provides information on the quantity and price at which market participants are willing to buy or sell, helping traders assess market liquidity and potential price movements.

Market Maker: A Market Maker is a financial institution or individual that provides liquidity to a market by continuously quoting both bid and ask prices for a specific financial instrument. Market makers ensure market liquidity and help facilitate smooth trading.

Market Manipulation: Market Manipulation refers to illegal or unethical practices that intentionally distort or manipulate market prices or trading activity. It can involve spreading false information, engaging in fraudulent trades, or creating artificial price movements.

Market Order: A Market Order67. Market Order: A Market Order is an order to buy or sell a financial instrument at the current market price. It is executed immediately at the best available price in the market. Market orders prioritize speed of execution over price, and the actual execution price may differ slightly from the expected price due to market fluctuations.

Market Sentiment: Market Sentiment refers to the overall attitude or opinion of market participants toward a particular financial instrument, sector, or the market as a whole. It is influenced by various factors, including economic conditions, news events, investor expectations, and market trends.

Momentum: Momentum is a technical analysis indicator that measures the speed and strength of a financial instrument's price movement over a specific period. It helps identify the rate of change and potential continuation of a trend, with higher momentum indicating stronger buying or selling pressure.

Momentum Oscillator: A Momentum Oscillator is a technical analysis tool that measures the momentum of a financial instrument. It compares the current price to a historical price point and generates an oscillator that oscillates above or below a centerline, providing insights into overbought and oversold conditions.

Monetary Policy: Monetary Policy refers to the actions taken by a central bank to manage and control a country's money supply, interest rates, and credit conditions. The objective of monetary policy is to achieve price stability, control inflation, promote economic growth, and maintain financial stability.

Moving Average: A Moving Average is a commonly used technical analysis tool that smooths out price fluctuations and reveals the underlying trend. It calculates the average price of a financial instrument over a specific period, providing a visual representation of the instrument's historical price performance.

Moving Average Convergence Divergence (MACD): Moving Average Convergence Divergence (MACD) is a popular technical analysis indicator that measures the relationship between two moving averages of a financial instrument's price. It helps identify potential trend reversals, momentum, and divergence between price and the indicator.

Options: Options are financial derivatives that give the buyer the right, but not the obligation, to buy (call option) or sell (put option) an underlying asset at a predetermined price within a specified time period. Options provide flexibility and can be used for speculation, hedging, or income generation.

Order: An Order is a request or instruction given by a trader to a broker or a trading platform to buy or sell a financial instrument. It specifies the price, quantity, and other relevant parameters for executing the desired trade.

Order Flow: Order Flow refers to the analysis and understanding of the incoming buy and sell orders for a particular financial instrument in the market. It involves studying the volume, direction, and speed of order placements to gain insights into market sentiment and potential price movements.

P/E Ratio (Price-to-Earnings Ratio): The Price-to-Earnings (P/E) Ratio is a valuation metric used to assess the relative value of a company's stock. It is calculated by dividing the current market price per share by the earnings per share (EPS) of the company. The P/E ratio helps investors gauge how much they are paying for each dollar of earnings.

PMI (Purchasing Managers' Index): The Purchasing Managers' Index (PMI) is an economic indicator that measures the activity level of purchasing managers in the manufacturing sector. It provides insights into business conditions, including new orders, production, employment, and supplier deliveries. A PMI reading above 50 indicates expansion, while below 50 indicates contraction.

Position: A Position refers to the ownership or exposure an investor or trader has in a particular financial instrument. It can be a long position (ownership) or a short position (borrowed or sold). The size and direction of a position determine the potential profit or loss based on market price movements.

Price Elasticity: Price elasticity in trading refers to the sensitivity of the quantity of a traded asset (such as stocks, commodities, or currencies) to changes in its price. It measures how responsive the demand or supply of an asset is to price changes. In simple terms, if an asset has high price elasticity, it means that small price changes can result in significant changes in trading volume. Conversely, if an asset has low price elasticity, price changes have a smaller impact on trading volume.

Relative Strength Index (RSI): The Relative Strength Index (RSI) is a popular momentum oscillator used in technical analysis. It measures the speed and change of price movements to determine overbought and oversold conditions. The RSI oscillates between 0 and 100, with readings above 70 indicating overbought and below 30 indicating oversold conditions.

Resistance: Resistance refers to a price level at which a financial instrument faces selling pressure, preventing further upward price movement. It is considered a psychological or technical barrier that may require significant buying pressure to overcome.

Resistance Level: Resistance Level is a specific price level at which a financial instrument has historically faced selling pressure and struggled to move beyond. It represents a significant hurdle that needs to be surpassed for a potential breakout to occur.

Revenue: Revenue, also known as sales or turnover, represents the total amount of money generated from the sale of goods or services by a company during a specific period. Revenue is a key measure of a company's top-line performance and is reported on its income statement.

Risk Appetite: Risk Appetite refers to an investor's or trader's willingness to take on risk in pursuit of potential returns. It reflects the level of comfort and tolerance for potential losses in their investment or trading activities.

Risk Management: Risk Management refers to the process of identifying, assessing, and mitigating potential risks associated with investment or trading activities. It involves implementing strategies and measures to control or minimize potential losses and protect capital.

Risk-Reward Ratio: Risk-Reward Ratio is a measure used to assess the potential return relative to the potential risk of an investment or trade. It compares the expected profit (reward) to the potential loss (risk), helping traders and investors evaluate the potential profitability and risk exposure of a trade or investment.

Scalable: Scalable refers to the characteristic of a system, strategy, or investment that can handle increasing volumes or sizes without a proportional loss in performance or efficiency. Scalable investments or strategies can be expanded or adjusted to accommodate larger positions or increased trading volumes.

Scalping: Scalping is a short-term trading strategy that aims to profit from small price movements in a financial instrument. Scalpers typically open and close trades within a short time frame, often seconds or minutes, to capture small increments in price.

Short Position: A Short Position is when a trader or investor sells a financial instrument that they do not own, expecting its price to decline. Profits are made by buying back the instrument at a lower price to cover the short position.

Short Squeeze: A Short Squeeze occurs when a significant upward price movement forces traders or investors who hold short positions to cover their positions by buying back the financial instrument. This buying pressure further drives up the price, resulting in potential losses for those with short positions.

Slippage: Slippage refers to the difference between the expected price of a trade and the actual price at which it is executed. It can occur during periods of high volatility or low liquidity, causing trades to be executed at a less favorable price than initially expected.

Spread: Spread refers to the difference between the bid price (selling price) and the ask price (buying price) of a financial instrument. It represents the transaction cost and reflects the liquidity and trading conditions of the market.

Stop Order: A Stop Order is an order to buy or sell a financial instrument once it reaches a specific price level, known as the stop price. Once the stop price is reached, the stop order becomes a market order and is executed at the best available price.

Stop-Loss Level: Stop-Loss Level is the predetermined price level at which a trader or investor intends to exit a position to limit potential losses. It is set below the entry price for long positions and above the entry price for short positions.

Stop-Loss Order: A Stop-Loss Order is an order placed by a trader or investor to automatically sell a financial instrument if its price reaches a specified stop-loss level. It is designed to limit potential losses by triggering an exit from the position if the price moves unfavorably.

Stop-Out Level: Stop-Out Level is the threshold at which a broker automatically closes a trader's position due to insufficient margin or equity in the trading account. It is set to protect both the trader and the broker from excessive losses.

Support: Support refers to a price level at which a financial instrument experiences buying pressure, preventing further downward price movement. It is considered a psychological or technical level that may require significant selling pressure to breach.

Support Level: Support Level is a specific price level at which a financial instrument has historically found buying support and rebounded from. It represents a significant level of demand that may act as a potential floor or turning point for the price.

Swing High: A Swing High refers to a peak or a high point reached by a financial instrument's price during a specific time period. It represents a temporary resistance level and marks the end of an upward swing or rally.

Swing Low: A Swing Low refers to a trough or a low point reached by a financial instrument's price during a specific time period. It represents a temporary support level and marks the end of a downward swing or decline.

Swing Trading: Swing Trading is a trading strategy that aims to capture shorter-term price movements within larger market trends. Swing traders seek to identify and capitalize on the swings or price fluctuations between established support and resistance levels.

Take-Profit Level: Take-Profit Level refers to a specific price level set by a trader or investor at which they intend to close a position and secure profits. It is a predetermined target price that the trader expects the financial instrument to reach.

Take-Profit Order: A Take-Profit Order is an order placed by a trader or investor to automatically close a position when the price reaches a specified take-profit level. It is used to lock in profits and exit a trade once the desired target price is reached.

Technical Analysis: Technical Analysis is a method of analyzing financial markets and making investment decisions based on the analysis of historical price patterns, trends, and statistical indicators. It involves studying charts, patterns, and technical indicators to forecast future price movements.

Trend: Trend refers to the general direction in which a financial instrument's price is moving over a specific period. It can be classified as an uptrend (rising prices), downtrend (falling prices), or sideways trend (range-bound prices).

Unemployment Rate: Unemployment Rate is a measure of the percentage of the labor force that is unemployed and actively seeking employment. It is an important economic indicator that reflects the health of the job market and the overall state of the economy.

Volatile: Volatile describes a financial instrument or market that experiences significant and rapid price fluctuations over a short period. Volatile markets are characterized by high price variability and can offer opportunities for traders and investors but also carry increased risks.

Volatility: Volatility is a statistical measure of the magnitude of price fluctuations or market movements for a financial instrument. It reflects the degree of uncertainty or risk associated with the instrument and is commonly used to assess the potential price range or volatility of an asset.

Volatility Index (VIX): The Volatility Index, commonly known as the VIX, is a popular measure of market volatility and investor sentiment. It is calculated based on the prices of options on the S&P 500 Index and is often referred to as the "fear gauge" as it tends to rise during periods of market uncertainty or stress.

Volatility Skew: Volatility Skew refers to the uneven or asymmetrical distribution of implied volatility across different strike prices of options. It indicates that market participants have different expectations or perceptions of future price movements for the underlying asset.

Volatility Smile: Volatility Smile refers to the graphical representation of implied volatility against strike prices in options pricing. It shows an asymmetrical pattern resembling a smile, indicating that options with different strike prices have different implied volatilities.

Whipsaw: Whipsaw refers to a situation in which the price of a financial instrument moves sharply in one direction, then quickly reverses and moves sharply in the opposite direction. Whipsaw movements can result in false signals and can be challenging for traders who try to anticipate price trends.

Yield: Yield refers to the income or return generated by an investment, typically expressed as an expectation for future economic conditions. It is the percentage of the investment amount. It can represent the interest, dividends, or other forms of income earned from holding a financial instrument.

Yield Curve: Yield Curve is a graphical representation of the interest rates or yields of bonds or other fixed-income securities plotted against their respective maturities. It shows the relationship between the short-term and long-term interest rates and can provide insights into the market.